A SEMANTIC AND STRUCTURAL ANALYSIS OF PHILEMON

A SEMANTIC AND STRUCTURAL ANALYSIS OF PHILEMON

John Banker

Summer Institute of Linguistics

© 1990, 1999 by the Summer Institute of Linguistics, Inc.
ISBN: 0-88312-934-5
Library of Congress Catalog Card Number: 90-070592
Printed in the United States of America

Summer Institute of Linguistics, Inc.
7500 W. Camp Wisdom Road
Dallas, TX 75236

CONTENTS

PREFACE 7
ABBREVIATIONS 8

GENERAL INTRODUCTION ....
    The Theory on Which a Semantic and Structural Analysis Is Based 9
    The Use of a Semantic and Structural Analysis 9
    Chart of Relations 11
    Chart of Paragraph Patrterns 12

INTRODUCTION TO THE SEMANTIC AND STRUCTURAL ANALYSIS OF PHILEMON ....
    The Participants in the Communication Situation 13
    The Occasion and Purpose of the Epistle 13
    The Genre and Style of the Epistle 13
    The Constituent Organization of the Epistle 14
    Overview: The Thematic Outline of the Epistle 15
    A Note on Hierarchical Structure 16

THE SEMANTIC UNITS OF PHILEMON ....
Philemon 1–25 (Epistle) 17
    Epistle Constituent 1–3 18
    Epistle Constituent 4–22 22
        Division Constituent 4–11 23
            Section Constituent 4–7 24
            Section Constituent 8–11 32
        Division Constituent 12–21 37
            Section Constituent 12–16 40
            Section Constituent 17 46
            Section Constituent 18–19 48
            Section Constituent 20 52
            Section Constituent 21 55
        Division Constituent 22 57
    Epistle Constituent 23–25 59

BIBLIOGRAPHY 62

PREFACE

As with various other *Semantic and Structural Analyses*, a number of people have been involved with the semantic analysis of Philemon, most notably Anthony Pope and John Werner. Anthony Pope did the original work on the analysis in 1977-78. Subsequently a committee, chaired by John Werner and including John Beekman, Michael Kopesec, and Robert Smith, continued the work. Sometime later I was assigned the responsibility of bringing the work to completion. Though I did an extensive revision including a number of changes in interpretation, much of the basic analysis remains the same. Also, I depended heavily on the earlier authors for discussion of textual problems, the communication situation, and the genre and style of the epistle. I appreciate very much each one who has been involved in the earlier work on the analysis of Philemon.

I am also grateful to Ellis Deibler and J. Harold Greenlee for their valuable review and comments in their respective fields of semantics and Greek. As for the production of this book, I would like to thank Betty Eastman for her many helpful suggestions in making the text more readable and Richard Blight for overseeing the many details of production. Thanks are also due Ron Olson for his direction and encouragement and to Elaine Beekman and Faith Blight for keyboarding this book.

As always, my wife, Betty, has given me daily support in innumerable ways, and without her I would have been unable to complete the work. She has also assisted me in editing the manuscript.

In closing, I pray that the One who has graciously enabled each of us in our contributions to this book will also enable each reader to benefit from it whether it is used in Bible translation or in the study of His Word in general.

ABBREVIATIONS

BAGD	Bauer, Arndt, Gingrich, and Danker (see bibliography)
KJV	King James Version
NEB	The New English Bible
NIV	The New International Version
RSV	Revised Standard Version
SSA	Semantic and Structural Analysis
TEV	Today's English Version
UBS	The United Bible Societies
(exc)	exclusive
(inc)	inclusive
MET	metaphor
MTY	metonymy
MS	manuscript
MSS	manuscripts
(pl)	plural
(sg)	singular
SYN	synecdoche
v.	verse
vv.	verses
*	a word being used in other than its primary meaning in contemporary English
**	see footnote (used only in text displays)

GENERAL INTRODUCTION

The theory on which *A Semantic and Structural Analysis* is based

This analytical commentary on Paul's letter to Philemon is based on a theory of semantic structure set forth in "The Semantic Structure of Written Communication" (Beekman, Callow, and Kopesec 1981). It has been prepared with the needs of the Bible translator particularly in view, though it should be useful to all serious students of God's Word. Like other commentaries, it aims to arrive at the meaning that the original writer intended to communicate to the original recipients. It differs from most other commentaries, however, in that it is consciously based on a theory of the structure of meaning. Consequently, a consistent and comprehensive approach to the analysis of the meaning is applied to the total document, whether that meaning is conveyed by the smallest segments of the written communication, such as words and their component parts, or whether it is conveyed by the largest segments, such as paragraphs and various combinations of paragraphs.

This *Semantic and Structural Analysis* (SSA) *of Philemon* does not include a detailed section on the theory and presentation of semantic and structural analyses as some of the earlier SSAs do (Colossians, 2 Thessalonians). The person who is building up his own collection of SSAs does not need this section to reappear in every SSA. So, for economy's sake, this section has been left out of the Philemon SSA, but the reader may refer to the Colossians or 2 Thessalonians SSA for this information. The Philemon SSA does, however, include a chart of relations and a chart of paragraph pattern subtypes for easy access to these important tools.

Each semantic unit of Philemon will be presented in a "display chart" showing the *structure* of the meaning. The relational structure appears at the left of the chart, and the referential contents to the right. The reader should note the following:

1. Italics are used in the display text to designate implicit material that has been made explicit. Note, however, that in some cases it is difficult to decide what is implicit material and what is actually a component of meaning of the Greek word being translated. Brackets are used to clarify references to antecedents; for example, 'him [Onesimus]'; 'this [16a]'.
2. An asterisk following a word indicates that the word is not being used in its primary meaning in contemporary English.
3. Each individual discussion note is set off by marking in bold type the word or phrase from the display text which is under discussion. The Greek text with literal English translation is not given in this SSA for each proposition as it was in some previous SSAs. Users of the SSA may refer to interlinear texts.

In this SSA a distinction is made between communication relations on the lower structural levels, paragraph pattern and macrostructure relations on the higher levels. The paragraph pattern relations have to do with genre and the macrostructure relations have to do with the overall patterning of the discourse. Thus the reader will find that a supportive paragraph in hortatory discourse which would have been labeled *grounds* in earlier SSAs is now labeled *basis*, and the corresponding supported paragraph will be called APPEAL rather than HEAD. For more information on paragraph patterns (or schema) see Tuggy 1992 and Kathleen Callow 1998:187–207.

The use of *A Semantic and Structural Analysis*

For the translator, who not only must determine the exegesis of a passage but also must determine how to resolve a myriad of translation problems, it sometimes becomes sheer drudgery to wade through the detailed reasoning backing up the exegetical decisions in the SSA or similar commentaries. On the other hand, the detailed reasoning is necessary to determine the best analysis. Any interpretation presented must be backed up with solid reasoning, and there is no way this can be done without adequate, detailed analysis, including reference to the Greek text. To discover whether or not the reasoning is solid, the translator must study the analysis which has been presented.

Does the translator who wants to use the SSA, then, have any other appropriate option than reading every part of the SSA? One approach is to use the display text of the SSA along with other commentaries, versions, and helps; and where there is obvious agreement, the translator may move ahead with confidence. Where there is a difference between the display and other texts, or there appears to be a number of alternatives, then the translator may consult the notes in the SSA on the particular verse or portion of a verse being studied in order to see what factors led to the decision represented in the display. The translator should then be better informed so that he can make his own *factually based* judgment as to the best interpretation. In some cases the notes will provide an alternate propositionalization which may occasionally appear to the translator to be the better solution. Also, since the SSA is prepared with the needs of the translator especially in mind, the notes of the SSA may supply needed information which is difficult to find elsewhere. If the translator is searching for such information as he works on a particular verse, it would be well for him to consult the SSA notes for that verse to see if the problem is dealt with.

Although the method of using the SSA described above is possible and helpful, nevertheless, in order to obtain the greatest benefit from an SSA, it should be read through in its entirety. Just as a part of any book or discourse is best understood in its complete context, so discussion of a single point in the SSA in many cases will best be understood if the user has maintained access to the context of the SSA as a whole.

Moreover, as will be seen from the following discussion, the display text and the notes work together to provide the information the translator needs for his work on any verse. Since the display text by its form is limited in the information it can provide, notes are provided that contribute to the fuller understanding of what the display text is seeking to communicate.

It should be understood that the SSA display text is not a translation in the common sense. It is a verbalization of *the analysis of the meaning* of the Greek text presented in propositional English surface structure form and with various restrictions. For instance, abstract nouns are avoided as much as possible, and the finite form of the verb is normally used in their place.

Words are used only in their primary senses. For "live" metaphors, the point of similarity (i.e., the full meaning of the figure intended to be communicated by the original author) is given in the display text. As a result, the display text does not always sound like natural, flowing English, as a good translation should. The addition of implicit material may make it sound too overloaded with information and too interpretative for a translation. Its primary purpose is to be a source of information, *not a model* for word-for-word translation into any real language. However, in some of its patterns it will more closely approximate patterns of many of the world's languages than normal English or Greek would. For example, if a language naturally uses abstract nouns in more or less the same way English or Greek does, it would be expected that translating using abstract nouns would in many cases (each case needs to be examined for itself) be more natural and effective than following the propositional form of the display text, in which abstract nouns are avoided. But if the language does not normally use abstract nouns, the propositional form of the display text may be helpful since it is built to give the translator the information he needs to turn abstract nouns into verbal constructions. At the same time, even in these languages a natural translation will avoid following the display text word for word; instead, it will follow its own patterns.

Chart of Relations

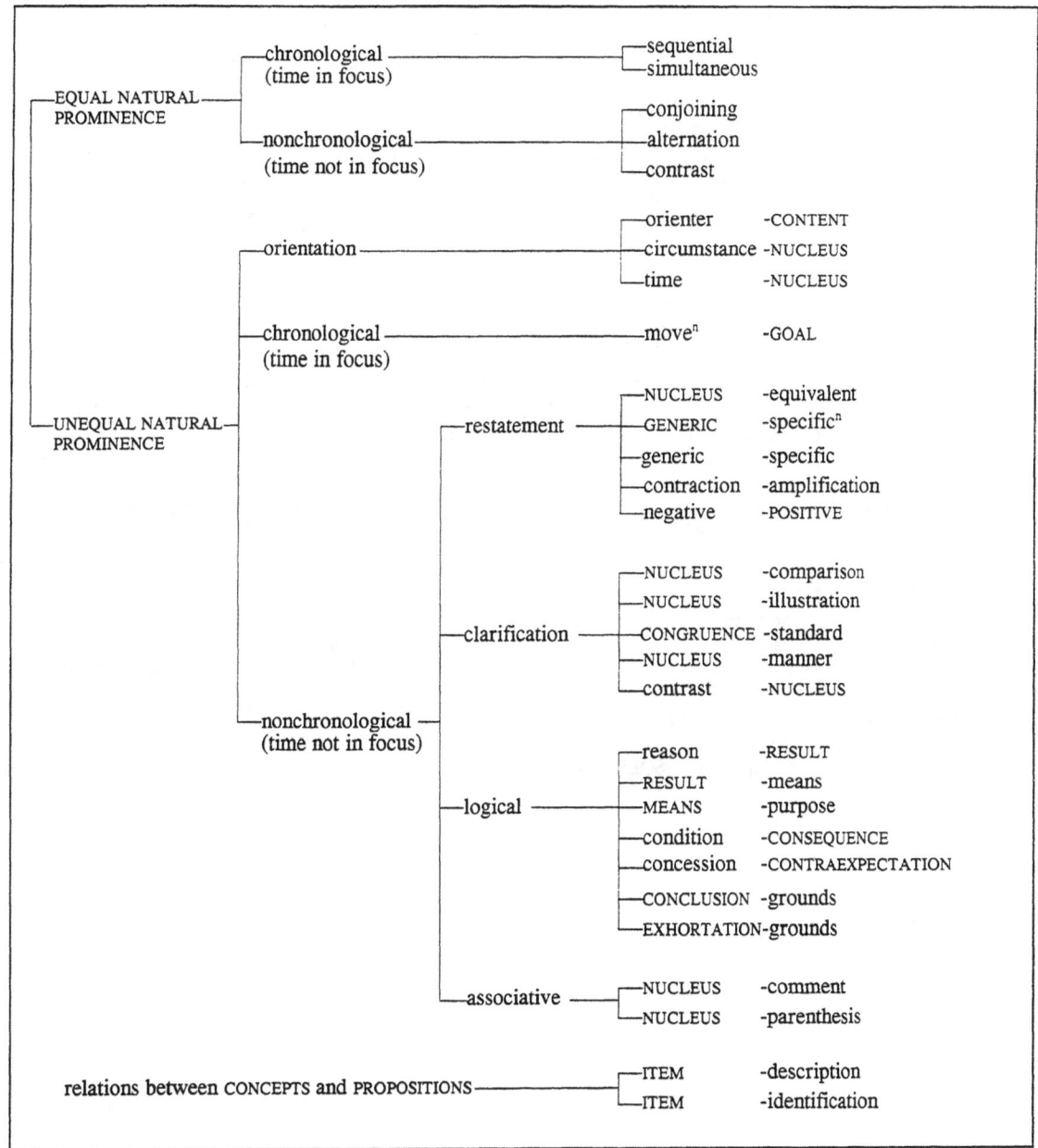

Notes on the Chart of Relations:

1. The relations are to be read horizontally, e.g., orienter-CONTENT, circumstance-NUCLEUS.
2. Since the Epistle to Philemon is nonnarrative, the narrative, or chronological, relations are not all included in this chart.
3. The relations are given in the order in which they are most commonly found in the Greek of the New Testament; thus an orienter usually precedes the CONTENT which it orients.
4. The naturally prominent member of a paired relation is shown in caps. There does not seem to be a natural head for contraction-amplification; the prominence will be determined by the context.
5. It should be noted that devices marking prominence can be used by the author to make the less prominent member of a pair as prominent as the one which is naturally prominent.

Paragraph-Pattern Types in Various Discourse Genres

(With a few exceptions one formula serves for each paragraph-pattern type; alternate formulas are separated by a semi-colon.)

		SOLUTIONALITY	CAUSALITY	VOLITIONALITY
IDEAS	EXPOSITORY −sequence	+problem (exp)+SOLUTION ±evidence^n ±(complication+SOLUTION) [(objection+REFUTATION)/ query+RESPONSE)]	+cause^n+EFFECT; +major+minor+INFER- ENCE; +evidence^n+INFERENCE; +PRINCIPLE+application^n	+justification^n+CLAIM
	NARRATIVE +sequence	+problem+RESOLUTION ±resolving incident^n ±(complication+RESOLUTION)	+occasion+OUTCOME	+step^n+GOAL
EMOTIONS	EXPRESSIVE −sequence	+problem (emo)+SOLUTION ±seeking/belief ±(complication+SOLUTION)	+situation^n+REACTION ±belief	+belief^n+CONTROL
	DESCRIPTIVE +sequence	+problem (dsc)+SOLUTION ±experience^n ±(complication+SOLUTION)	+situation^n+REACTION	+description^n+DECLAR- ATION
BEHAVIOR	HORTATORY −sequence	+problem (hrt)+APPEAL ±basis^n ±(complication+SOLUTION)	+basis^n+APPEAL; +APPEAL+application^n; +basis^n+COMMISSIVE	+motivation+ENABLE- MENT^n; +motivation^n+APPEAL
	PROCEDURAL +sequence	+problem (prc)+SOLUTION ±step^n ±(complication+SOLUTION)	+APPEAL+outcome	+STEP^n+accomplishment

INTRODUCTION TO THE SEMANTIC AND STRUCTURAL ANALYSIS OF PHILEMON

The participants in the communication situation

The identification of the author and addressees occurs at the beginning of the letter along with a wish for the well-being of the addressees (1–3). This is the general practice in Greco-Roman letters. (Cf. the opening of Major Claudius Lysias' letter to Governor Felix in Acts 23:26.) At first it may seem that there are two authors—Paul and Timothy—and four addressees —Philemon, Apphia, Archippus, and the congregation of believers that meets in Philemon's (or Archippus') home. But the first- and second-person pronouns used in the body of the letter are all in the singular except for two occurrences of 'you' in the plural in v. 22. All first- and second-person verb endings are singular as well, as are the vocative forms. Also, the author identifies himself exclusively as Paul in vv. 9 and 19. So there is no doubt that Paul is the author of the letter; his inclusion of Timothy's name signals that Timothy is with him and is in agreement with what Paul says in the letter.

The use of the second-person *singular* pronoun in v. 4, without any other reference there as to who the addressee is, means that there has been some earlier signal to point out who among the three individuals addressed is the primary recipient. That signal might be found in the order in which the addressees are written down and/or in a separate notation at the beginning of the letter such as πρός 'to' plus the name, even as πρὸς Φιλήμονα 'to Philemon' has appeared in Greek texts for centuries. (If it were known that πρὸς Φιλήμονα actually did appear in the original manuscript, then πρὸς Φιλήμονα would be part of the total discourse.)

Apphia cannot be the primary recipient referred to by the second-person singular pronouns in the body of the letter since the primary recipient is called ἀδελφέ 'brother' in vv. 7 and 20, while she, of course, is referred to as τῇ ἀδελφῇ 'sister'. Of the other two, the common opinion or assumption has been that the primary recipient is Philemon, though a few commentators have argued for Archippus. The fact that Archippus stands third in the list of the four entities addressed does not give much support for his being the primary recipient. Neither can the witness of tradition be easily dismissed.

But if only one of the addressees is meant as the primary recipient, what is Paul's intention in addressing the other two individuals and the house church? In a way, it may seem that Paul's mention of the other names is little more than sending greetings, but the grammatical signals he uses are those that normally designate recipients, not greetings. Commentators see the address to Apphia, Archippus, and all who meet in the home as necessary because they will all be involved in helping Philemon carry out Paul's request of receiving Onesimus in a loving, Christian way. The major responsibility, of course, rests with Philemon, the slave's owner.

Philemon's slave, Onesimus, is mentioned as 'one of you' in Col. 4:9. It may be inferred, therefore, that Philemon lived in the city of Colossae.

The occasion and purpose of the epistle

A slave (16) by the name of Onesimus (10), who belongs to Philemon, has run away, an act punishable in the Roman Empire at the discretion of the slave's owner. Death was one of the owner's options. Onesimus may have stolen some of his master's money or in some other way defrauded him (18). He has come in contact with Paul, and Paul has led him to Christ (10). Paul has become very fond of him (12), and Onesimus has become a useful helper to Paul (11). However, Paul will not keep him without Philemon's consent (14) and so is sending him back (12) with this accompanying letter. Paul's major concern is that Philemon will receive Onesimus as a dear Christian brother rather than as a slave (16), that he will receive him even as he would Paul himself (17).

The genre and style of the epistle

In line with its purpose to move Philemon to welcome the returning runaway slave as if he were Paul himself, this epistle fits the genre of the Greco-Roman letter of recommendation, of which there are examples among the papyri. The main section (4–22) follows the prescriptions of the Greco-Roman writers on the art of persuasion. Its introductory material is designed to dispose the reader favorably toward the author (4–9). It continues with an appeal to the intellect (10–19), including the countering of objections (18–19). Then comes the appeal to the emotions (20), followed by closing remarks (21–22). (Note that while most of these units equate with the constituent organization proposed in this SSA, for various reasons which will be discussed later they do not all equate.)

Probably because of the delicacy of the situation, Paul delays mention of the name of Onesimus as long as he possibly can, even after he has begun to describe him. He also delays the statement of the request (17b) until after he has stated most of the major grounds for it.

Paul's plays on words help set the tone of his letter. The word ὀναίμην 'may I be profited' (20) is from the same root as the name Ὀνήσιμος 'Profitable'. The use of ἄχρηστος 'useless' and εὔχρηστος 'useful' (11) is a play on words involving the same meaning as that of Onesimus' name. Some would even propose that it is possible that ἄχρηστος and εὔχρηστος suggested ἄχριστος 'Christless' and εὔχριστος 'Christful', since the diachronic Greek phonetic process of itacism had already brought η and ι close to each other in pronunciation.

The Constituent Organization of the Epistle

```
                          PHILEMON 1–25
|                             Epistle                              |

EC 1–3                        EC 4–22                       EC 23–25
| Para |                    | Division |                   | Para |

       DC 4–11                    DC 12–21              DC 22
     | Section |                 | Section |          | Para |

     SC 4–7   SC 8–11  SC 12–16  SC 17  SC 18–19  SC 20   SC 21
     | Para | Para  |  Pr Cl  | Para |  Pr Cl  | Pr Cl | Pr Cl |
```

Abbreviations: EC   Epistle Constituent
                 DC   Division Constituent
                 SC   Section Constituent
                 Para   Paragraph
                 Pr Cl   Propositional Cluster

INTRODUCTION

OVERVIEW: THE THEMATIC OUTLINE OF THE EPISTLE

PHILEMON 1–25 (Epistle) THEME: Onesimus is as dear to me as my own self (and should now be even dearer to you than he is to me); therefore, please receive him as you would receive me. I will repay to you whatever he owes you.

EPISTLE CONSTITUENT 1–3 (Paragraph: Opening of the epistle) I, Paul, am writing this letter to you, Philemon, and those with you. May God bless you(pl).

EPISTLE CONSTITUENT 4–22 (Division: Body of the epistle) Onesimus is as dear to me as my own self (and should now be even dearer to you than he is to me); therefore, please receive him as you would receive me. I will repay to you whatever he owes you.

> **DIVISION CONSTITUENT 4–11** (Section: Introduction of the body) I thank God very much for your love for God's people. Therefore, since I know that you love them, I request rather than command you to do what you ought to do for my spiritual son Onesimus.
>
>> **SECTION CONSTITUENT 4–7** (Paragraph: Evidence for 8–11) I thank God and rejoice greatly because you have shown that you love God's people.
>>
>> **SECTION CONSTITUENT 8–11** (Paragraph: Inference of 4–7) Since I know that you love God's people, I request rather than command you to do what you ought to do for my spiritual son Onesimus.
>
> **DIVISION CONSTITUENT 12–21** (Section: Nucleus of the body) Onesimus is as dear to me as my own self (and should now be even dearer to you than he is to me); therefore, please receive him as you would receive me. I will repay to you whatever he owes you.
>
>> **SECTION CONSTITUENT 12–16** (Paragraph: Basis$_1$ for the appeal of 17) I am sending Onesimus back to you. He is as dear to me as my own self, and he will now be even dearer to you than he is to me.
>>
>> **SECTION CONSTITUENT 17** (Propositional Cluster: Appeal for 12–21) If you consider me your partner, receive Onesimus as you would receive me.
>>
>> **SECTION CONSTITUENT 18–19** (Paragraph: Basis$_2$ for the appeal of 17) I guarantee to repay to you whatever Onesimus owes you.
>>
>> **SECTION CONSTITUENT 20** (Propositional Cluster: Basis$_3$ for the appeal of 17) Please encourage me in this matter as you encourage other believers in Christ.
>>
>> **SECTION CONSTITUENT 21** (Propositional Cluster: Basis$_4$ for the appeal of 17) I have written this letter to you confident of your compliance with my request.
>
> **DIVISION CONSTITUENT 22** (Paragraph: Closure of the body) Also, keep a guest room ready for me.

EPISTLE CONSTITUENT 23–25 (Paragraph: Closing of the epistle) Epaphras and my other fellow workers greet you(sg). May the Lord Jesus Christ bless you(pl) spiritually.

A note on hierarchical structure

The composition of this epistle points out very clearly that instead of each higher-level constituent having only one role, some of the constituents may have more than one role. For example, assume a certain composition has three units which we will label A, B, and C, and which occur in that order. If unit B has a clear relationship with unit A and an equally clear though different relationship with unit C, but unit A and unit C cannot be related to one another even through B, then a cut must be made somewhere. A decision must be made as to whether to cut between A and B, with B and C forming a unit on the next higher level, or between B and C, with A and B forming a unit on the next higher level.

One case in point in Philemon involves units 4–7, 8–11, and 12–16. Unit 4–7 at first appears to be one of Paul's typical thanksgiving and prayer units, and as such would stand alone as an introduction to the body (i.e., to the main part of the body) of the epistle. But the presence of logical reasoning between 4–7 and 8ff., which διό 'therefore' at the beginning of v. 8 helps to signal, shows that there is really an evidence-inference relationship between 4–7 and 8ff. On the other hand, 8–11 is already beginning to deal with components of the hortatory unit which basically makes up the rest of the body of the epistle. Verses 8–9 state that the exhortation will be a mitigated one, while 10–11 state the topic of the hortatory unit, Onesimus. Does unit 8–11 relate more closely to unit 4–7 or to unit 12–16? The analyst may go around and around in circles trying to find the correct answer. But is there really a correct answer or is the problem that here there is structural organization that cannot be handled by our present SSA labeling or diagramming system? It is similar to attempting to handle three-dimensional objects on a two-dimensional plane. Things just don't fit. In a situation such as this, the answer seems to be to take all the important factors into consideration and make a cut where it seems best but realize that, in cutting, one is doing so because of the constraints of the present system and there is no completely "correct" answer as to where the cut should be.

Another place where the organization of the epistle does not exactly fit the present SSA system is in v. 17. The main clause of 17 is the major *APPEAL* of the hortatory section of the epistle, with four *basis* units supporting it. But 17a essentially has the same role as these basis units, though it is grammatically a dependent clause of 17b. In earlier work done on the structural analysis of Philemon by others, a high-level cut was made between 17a and 17b. However, the cut in this present analysis is made between 16 and 17 in order not to assign two parts of a close-knit grammatical sentence to different higher-level semantic units.

A third, though probably not so significant, example is found in vv. 21–22. Both verses appear to deal somewhat with rapport, but there are other reasons for classifying 21 as a final *basis* of the hortatory unit and 22 as a *closure* of the body.

THE SEMANTIC UNITS OF PHILEMON
PHILEMON 1–25 (Epistle)

THEME: Onesimus is as dear to me as my own self (and should now be even dearer to you than he is to me); therefore, please receive him as you would receive me. I will repay to you whatever he owes you.

¶MACROSTRUCTURE	CONTENTS
opening	1–3 I, Paul, am writing this letter to you, Philemon, and those with you. May God bless you(pl).
BODY	4–22 Onesimus is as dear to me as my own self (and should now be even dearer to you than he is to me); therefore, please receive him as you would receive me. I will repay to you whatever he owes you.
closing	23–25 Epaphras and my other fellow workers greet you(sg). May the Lord Jesus Christ bless you(pl) spiritually.

See p. 18 for vv. 1–3; p. 22 for vv. 4–22; p. 59 for vv. 23–25.

STRUCTURE OF THE EPISTLE

The Epistle to Philemon has the three characteristic parts of a Pauline epistle: the *opening* (address and blessing), the BODY (the basic message Paul wants to communicate), and the *closing* (final greetings and benediction).

EPISTLE CONSTITUENT 1-3 (Paragraph: Opening of the epistle)

THEME: I, Paul, am writing this letter to you, Philemon, and those with you. May God bless you(pl).

STRUCTURE	CONTENTS
ADDRESS — NUCLEUS₁ — description	1a *I, Paul, am* a prisoner *who serves* Christ Jesus;
ADDRESS — NUCLEUS₁ — 'I, Paul'	1b *I,* together with Timothy, *our(inc)* brother,* *am writing this letter* to *you(sg)*, Philemon, *our(exc)* dear *friend* and fellow worker.
ADDRESS — NUCLEUS₂	2a *I am also writing to you(sg)*, Apphia, *our(exc)* sister,* and to *you(sg)*, Archippus, *who are like* our(exc) fellow soldier, *because you(sg) serve Christ steadfastly, together with us(exc)*.
ADDRESS — NUCLEUS₃	2b *I am also writing* to the group of believers *which meets* in your(sg) house, *Philemon*.
BLESSING	3 *We(exc) pray that* God our(inc) Father and *our(inc)* Lord Jesus Christ *will continue to* act graciously toward you(pl) and *will continue to* cause you(pl) to have peace/be peaceful.*

See p. 22 for vv. 4–22.

BOUNDARIES AND COHERENCE

The initial boundary of this unit coincides with the beginning of the epistle discourse. Verses 1-3 are very characteristic of the opening unit in Paul's other epistles and somewhat similar to the openings of other letters of the time. Verses 1-3 are similar grammatically to Paul's other epistle openings in that there are no verbs at all in these three verses. The first verb in the epistle, εὐχαριστῶ 'I thank' at the very beginning of v. 4, marks the beginning of the next unit, the BODY of the EPISTLE.

Also characteristic of the opening of a letter is the identification of the writer and those with him in the nominative case (Paul and Timothy) and the addressees in the dative case (Philemon, Apphia, Archippus, and the local house church). This is typically followed by the blessing, which is characteristically the last part of the opening.

PROMINENCE AND THEME

The ADDRESS and the BLESSING have distinctive roles in the *opening* of the epistle, and they are related by conjoining rather than being in a supportive relationship, so the theme must be drawn from both of them. As far as the ADDRESS is concerned, it is our view that Paul is the basic author of the epistle (rather than Paul and Timothy being full co-authors), while Philemon is the basic recipient (since he alone is addressed in the body of the epistle). Therefore, only Paul and Philemon are mentioned by name in the theme statement. However, some reference must be made to the other recipients since in the blessing Paul asks God to bless them all (ὑμῖν 'you(pl)'), so they are referred to as 'those with you'.

As for the BLESSING, it seems best to follow the Colossians SSA (John Callow 1983:25) and use 'God' to refer to the Godhead and 'bless' to refer to granting of both grace and peace. 'May' is substituted for '*we(exc) pray*'.

NOTES

1a *I*, Paul, *am* a prisoner *who serves* Christ Jesus The RSV translation 'a prisoner for Christ Jesus' is not as literal as it may sound since the Greek text is a genitive construction, δέσμιος Χριστοῦ Ἰησοῦ '(a) prisoner of Christ Jesus'. It is very difficult to know exactly what Paul intended by this expression. The first thing to be said is that Paul is an actual prisoner (confined either in some type of prison or chained to a guard in a private home as in Acts 28), and the context of the whole epistle strongly suggests that this is what Paul is focusing on here rather than this being a wholly figurative expression. Thus the propositionalization should focus on the reality of his physical imprisonment rather than on the figurative relationship.

Secondly, it must be determined whether the genitive construction basically signals an action in which Christ is the agent or in which Paul is the agent. Is the sense intended that Christ willed or appointed Paul to be a prisoner, or that Paul is a prisoner who serves Christ Jesus (or because he serves Christ Jesus, as RSV would suggest). Note that in 2 Tim. 1:11-12a Paul states, "For this gospel I was appointed a preacher and apostle and teacher, and therefore I suffer as I do" (RSV). In 2 Tim. 1:8 he says, "Do not be ashamed then of testifying to our Lord, nor of me his prisoner, but take your share of suffering for the gospel in the power of God" (RSV). In 2 Tim. 2:9 Paul says, "the gospel for which I am suffering and wearing fetters, like a criminal" (RSV). In 2 Tim., then, Paul's role as prisoner of the Lord is not stated as an appointment but is viewed as something done for the gospel and thus for the Lord. This would also seem to be the sense of δέσμιος Χριστοῦ Ἰησοῦ 'prisoner of Christ Jesus' in Phlm. 9 (see the discussion on that verse).

Note that if we take Christ as the agent in the genitive construction 'prisoner of Christ Jesus' but focus not on the initiating action ('willed' or 'appointed' or 'imprisoned by') but on the continuing action, 'I am held captive by Christ Jesus', then the sense communicated would be the figurative sense, which we have said is not in focus as much as the physical sense. However, 'serve' may function as a reciprocal of 'hold captive'. Based on all the above considerations, using 'serve' would seem to be a good solution: '*I, Paul, am* a prisoner *who serves* Christ Jesus'.

An alternative would be to propositionalize as '*I, Paul, am* a prisoner *because I serve* Christ Jesus' where 'because' not only indicates the reason for his being put in prison but also indicates the beneficiary of his imprisonment. That is, this is a normal propositionalization for such expressions as 'for the sake of'—'for the sake of Christ Jesus, for Christ Jesus'. This, then, is similar to 'who serves Christ Jesus'. The latter is used in the display text here because it seems to be stating the more basic relationship in the genitive construction 'prisoner of Christ Jesus', avoiding explicit reference to cause.

The ordering of the propositions in 1a–b in the display text was chosen because it was felt to be less disjointed than other orders that might have been selected. It basically follows the order of the Greek text. In some languages reference to the writing may need to come first.

1b *I*, together with Timothy How much input, if any, did Timothy have in the content of the letter? After mentioning Timothy at the very beginning of the letter, Paul never explicitly includes him again, not even with the use of 'we' (as he does sometimes in Colossians, for instance); so one wonders how much input, if any, Timothy had in the actual wording of the letter. No doubt he agreed with Paul's general principles in writing the letter, and this may be the significant point. Even though Paul had full authority as an apostle of Christ and even though Timothy himself was not an apostle, it would seem that Timothy's name along with Paul's at the very beginning of the letter, where validity and authority were usually established, would give weight to what Paul was saying.

Note that Timothy is distinguished from Paul's other fellow workers (cf. vv. 23–24) by being mentioned at the very beginning of the letter. Note also that he is mentioned in this same place in five other epistles. In three of them he is the only other person mentioned in this position (2 Cor., Phil., Col.), and in two of them he is mentioned with Silas (1 and 2 Thess.). Lohse (1968:189) says, "The fact that an associate is mentioned also calls attention to the authoritative character of the letter. Timothy is at the apostle's side as a trustworthy Christian brother.... The associate, however, plays no role in the formulation of the letter."

It seems best to follow the Colossians SSA (John Callow 1983:25–26) here and use 'together with' along with the singular form of the verb: '*I, together with Timothy, our(inc) brother,* am writing this letter to you(sg), Philemon*'. 'Together with' shows the unity in purpose, while the singular form of the verb shows that basically it is Paul who is the letter's author. (It is acknowledged, however, that this type of construction might be difficult, if not impossible, to produce in some languages. In those cases it may be best to state both Paul and Timothy as the agents of the writing of the letter in vv. 1–2 and let the context of the body of the letter, which clearly indicates that only Paul is its author, carry that information, unless, of course, some other way can be found to handle it.)

Timothy, *our(inc)* brother* There is no evidence that ὁ ἀδελφός 'the brother' here means anything but Christian brother in a rather broad sense. The asterisk indicates that it is used in this special Christian sense rather than in the biological sense, which is the primary sense in English. 'Our' is added since many languages, even English, must have an indication to whom one is related as a brother. Since 'brother' is used in this broad Christian sense, the inclusive form of the pronoun would be the appropriate form.

am writing this letter There are no verbs at all in the Greek text of vv. 1–3, but verbs must be used in the propositionalization. What is the implied action in Παῦλος ... Φιλήμονι ...

καὶ Ἀπφίᾳ . . . καὶ Ἀρχίππῳ . . . καὶ τῇ κατ' οἶκόν σου ἐκκλησίᾳ 'Paul . . . to Philemon . . . and to Apphia . . . and to Archippus . . . and to the church in your(sg) house'? In the propositionalization of Philemon in *Translating the Word of God* (Beekman and Callow 1974:363), 'greet' was used here. However, note that in Greek the verb ἀσπάζομαι 'greet' takes the accusative to indicate those being greeted, while all the aforementioned people are referred to in the dative case.

Other things being equal, the most natural verb to use here is 'write'. Verse 21 would seem to bear this out for Greek: 'confident of your obedience, I have written (ἔγραψα) to you'. Also, γράφω 'I write' is appropriate to the nominative and dative cases used in the Greek text of vv. 1-2. There is little doubt that 'write' is the appropriate word in English too, but it must be remembered that Paul himself did not do the actual penning of most of the letter (see notes on v. 19) and that Timothy, who is included as being involved somehow in the implied action, perhaps had limited input in composing the letter. For these reasons, John Callow (1983:25–26) prefers to use 'send' instead of 'write' in the similar case in Colossians. And this is a good alternative. It is not used here since 'write' seems to be the more natural word in this context.

Philemon, our(exc) dear *friend* and fellow worker The phrase τῷ ἀγαπητῷ καὶ συνεργῷ ἡμῶν might be translated either as 'our beloved fellow worker' or 'our beloved *friend* and fellow worker'. That is, ἀγαπητῷ 'beloved' might be taken as a substantive, 'beloved one, beloved friend', or as an adjective modifying συνεργῷ 'fellow worker'. The fact that in the propositionalization a noun must be chosen for 'beloved' to modify and there is, in fact, already present a noun that grammatically may be the one that 'beloved' was intended to modify, might suggest that the best solution would be to propositionalize as 'our(exc) beloved fellow worker'. But the use of καί 'and' between τῷ ἀγαπητῷ 'beloved' and συνεργῷ 'fellow worker' suggests that Paul wants to stress both of these descriptions of Philemon. To maintain this emphasis, it seems better to propositionalize as 'our(exc) dear/beloved *friend* and fellow worker'.

'Our' most likely refers to Paul and Timothy, since they are in the immediate context. 'Our' modifies both 'dear *friend*' and 'fellow worker'. 'Dear' is used in the display text instead of 'beloved' since it is more natural in modern English. Alternate propositionalizations would be: 'our(exc) *friend whom* we(exc) love and *who is* our(exc) fellow worker', 'our(exc) fellow worker *whom* we(exc) love', '*you(sg) are a friend whom* we(exc) love and *you(sg)* work together with us(exc)'.

2a Apphia, *our(exc)* sister* 'Sister', like 'brother', is asterisked because it refers to the specialized sense of a Christian sister in the Lord. Many commentators think that Apphia is the wife of Philemon. This seems plausible since Paul is dealing with a family matter, the return of one of the servants in the household. It is much easier to explain why Paul would include Philemon's wife as a recipient of the letter than it is to seek some other reason for a woman being addressed.

Archippus Is Archippus the son of Philemon and Apphia? There is no solid evidence for this assumption, though many commentators suggest it and it has been mentioned by commentators from very early times based on the likelihood that a single determining factor guides the listing of the recipients of a letter. Since Apphia quite likely is Philemon's wife and since the matter being discussed in the letter is one that concerns the whole family, Archippus is probably a family member as well. However, Paul's statement in Col. 4:17, "And say to Archippus, 'See that you fulfil the ministry which you have received in the Lord'" (RSV), suggests that Archippus may have had some position in the local church, and this may have been as a leader in the local church that met in Philemon's house.

who are like **our(exc) fellow soldier,** *because you(sg) serve Christ steadfastly, together with us(exc)* It is obvious that 'fellow soldier' is a metaphor since Paul was not a real soldier and there is no evidence that Archippus was either. The question that must be asked is, What grounds of comparison did Paul intend here when he stated that Archippus was a fellow soldier? Since we know little about Archippus and his situation, we lack a specific context into which we might fit Paul's designation of 'fellow soldier'. The only other mention of Archippus is (as already noted) in Col. 4:17 where Paul says, "And say to Archippus, 'See that you fulfil the ministry which you have received in the Lord'" (RSV).

The best way to answer the question about intended grounds of comparison, then, is to examine other references where Paul uses the 'soldier' metaphor to see if he mentions grounds of comparison in these cases. One of these would be 2 Tim. 2:3, where Paul states, "Endure hardship with us like a good soldier of Christ Jesus" (NIV). He goes on to say in v. 4, "No one serving as a soldier gets involved in civilian affairs—he wants to please his commanding officer." In Eph. 6:10–17, Paul compares the Christian to a soldier by the following phrases: 'strong in the Lord', putting on 'the whole armor of God' that he 'may be able to stand' in the day of battle. This ability to stand will be the result of complete dependence on God's armor and full commitment to stand firm (Eph. 6:13). In Phlm. 2a, it seems best to use as grounds of comparison that characteristic in the preceding passages which is most generic and occurs most often. This would seem to be endurance and steadfastness. The following propositionalization has been chosen: '*who are like* our(exc) fellow soldier, *because you(sg) serve Christ steadfastly together with us(exc)*'. Note that steadfastness and endurance presuppose hardship and difficulty and, in fact, in some languages can only be referred to with explicit mention of hardship.

2b your(sg) house The evidence is not all that conclusive as to whether 'your' (singular in Greek) refers to Philemon or Archippus, though it may be better to understand the church as meeting in Philemon's house rather than that of Archippus, since 'your(sg)' is possibly most naturally taken as referring to the main recipient of the letter. The opinion of the great majority of commentators is that 'your' refers to Philemon.

3 *We(exc) pray that* It is probably better to use 'we' rather than 'I' as the agent of the implied prayer since Paul has mentioned both himself and Timothy in the opening and has used ἡμῶν 'we' twice in the opening (τῷ ἀγαπητῷ καὶ συνεργῷ ἡμῶν 'our beloved *friend* and fellow worker'; τῷ συστρατιώτῃ ἡμῶν 'our fellow soldier') where he might have used μου 'my'. Note that the implied 'we' here in v. 3 is dual.

***will continue to* act graciously toward you(pl)** Following the *Semantic Structure Analysis of Second Thessalonians* (John Callow 1982:24), this verse is regarded as a prayer "expressed in a brief and stylized form." The abstract noun χάρις 'grace' needs to be changed into verbal form for the propositionalization. Two options present themselves, options that one often encounters in translation. The first is to use a verb in English that basically carries the same meaning in this context as the Greek abstract noun. If this cannot be found, then the second option is to use a verb phrase that is either commonly used in English to represent the same meaning as that of χάρις or could by common consent (and subsequent teaching) be understood to have reference to that meaning. As for the first option, the word 'bless' seems a potential candidate. It is difficult to know which one of the several senses of 'bless' is the primary sense but the sense "to invoke God's favor upon (a person or thing)" *(The Reader's Digest Great Encyclopedic Dictionary* 1966, entry number four) seems quite close to the meaning of χάρις in this context. John Callow states in his comments on χάρις in the 2 Thess. SSA (p. 24) that "There is not as much difference as would appear at first sight" between "the full theological sense of God giving his blessings freely to those who can in no way merit them" and "the more general sense of 'bless', 'do good to', 'act kindly towards'," since, "for Paul, 'grace' is the word that characterizes all God's favorable attitudes and actions towards sinful men." Callow, however, chooses to use that which has been referred to above as a second option (a verb phrase), 'act graciously'. It would seem to me that either 'bless' or 'act graciously' could be used here.

cause you(pl) to have peace/be peaceful* Regarding εἰρήνη 'peace', John Callow (ibid.) says, "It is very widely held that the choice of this word reflects the Hebrew greeting of *shalom* 'peace', which expresses much more than lack of strife, or even inner peacefulness. Rather it conveys the idea of 'spiritual prosperity', 'enjoying God's blessing', general 'blessedness'. In other words, it is the reciprocal of God's blessing, the recipients' state of blessedness." The asterisk on 'peace/be peaceful' indicates that the word is to be understood in a specialized way.

EPISTLE CONSTITUENT 4–22 (Division: Body of the epistle)

THEME: Onesimus is as dear to me as my own self (and should now be even dearer to you than he is to me); therefore, please receive him as you would receive me. I will repay to you whatever he owes you.

MACROSTRUCTURE	CONTENTS
introduction	4–11 I thank God very much for your love for God's people. Therefore, since I know that you love them, I request rather than command you to do what you ought to do for my spiritual son Onesimus.
NUCLEUS	12–21 Onesimus is as dear to me as my own self (and should now be even dearer to you than he is to me); therefore, please receive him as you would receive me. I will repay to you whatever he owes you.
closure	22 Also, keep a guest room ready for me.

See p. 23 for vv. 4–11; p. 37 for vv. 12–21; p. 57 for v. 22.

BOUNDARIES AND COHERENCE

The initial boundary has been discussed under 1–3. As for the final boundary, final greetings are characteristic of the closing in Paul's epistles. They begin in Philemon with the first word of v. 23, ἀσπάζεται 'he greets'. Although it is possible that a case could be made for including Paul's announcement of his proposed visit to Philemon in the *closing*, it is considered in this analysis as having a closer connection with the *BODY* of the letter.

PROMINENCE AND THEME

The theme of the *NUCLEUS*, of course, should be the basic part of the theme statement for the division. Since the *introduction* deals with rapport and only introduces the topic, i.e., Onesimus, no part of it is included in the theme (except for Onesimus' name). The *closure* has been analyzed as having a basic function of rapport so is excluded from the division theme statement.

DIVISION CONSTITUENT 4–11 (Section: Introduction of the body)

THEME: I thank God very much for your love for God's people. Therefore, since I know that you love them, I request rather than command you to do what you ought to do for my spiritual son Onesimus.

MACROSTRUCTURE	CONTENTS
EVIDENCE	4–7 I thank God and rejoice greatly because you have shown that you love God's people.
INFERENCE	8–11 Therefore, since I know that you love God's people, I request rather than command you to do what you ought to do for my spiritual son Onesimus.

See p. 24 for vv. 4–7; p. 32 for vv. 8–11.

BOUNDARIES AND COHERENCE

The initial boundary has been discussed under the opening of the epistle.

Verses 4–7 are characteristic of Paul's introductions in other epistles with the typical thanksgiving and prayer. Here the situations calling forth the thanksgiving (v. 5) and the situation for Paul's joy and encouragement (v. 7) both deal with Philemon's love for God's people so that a 'sandwich' structure is formed with the content of the prayer in the middle (v. 6). Verses 8ff. do not deal with thanksgiving and prayer but are more introductory to the hortatory section which makes up the major part of the epistle, stating the type of genre (παρακαλῶ 'I request') and the participant who is the topic of the discourse, Onesimus.

Since vv. 8ff. deal with these aspects that are closely related to the hortatory unit, on first thought it would seem that the introductory unit of thanksgiving and prayer would not have a close tie with 8ff. However, v. 8 begins with the connective διό 'therefore', signaling a connection between 4–7 and what follows. Verses 8ff. are an *INFERENCE* based on vv. 4–7. Since Philemon has shown that he loves all God's saints, therefore Paul would rather request him to do something for one of God's saints than command him to do so.

As for the final boundary, after v. 8 there are no clear grammatical signals of a paragraph break until the οὖν 'therefore' at the beginning of 17. However, semantically there is a major change in function at the beginning of 12. From 12 on, Paul begins his direct support for the *APPEAL* in 17. The *APPEAL* in 17b, 'Therefore . . . receive him as you would receive me', is the reciprocal of 'I am sending him back to you' of 12a. In contrast to this, vv. 8–11, as mentioned, introduce the type of discourse, hortatory schema, stating that it is a mild hortatory type, and then introduce the topic of the discourse, Onesimus.

Also, the fact that vv. 4–7 are tied logically to vv. 8–11 prevents connecting 12–16 to 8–11 as all one paragraph. (For more discussion on this subject, see "A Note on Hierarchical Structure" on p. 16.)

PROMINENCE AND THEME

With paragraph-pattern-type units, elements from both constituents characteristically form the theme of the unit.

SECTION CONSTITUENT 4–7 (Paragraph: Evidence for 8–11)

THEME: I thank God and rejoice greatly because you have shown that you love God's people.

¶ PTRN	RELATIONAL STRUCTURE	CONTENTS
REACTION₁	NUCLEUS	4a I always thank my God (or, God whom I worship)
	circumstance	4b when I pray for you,** *Philemon*,
situation₁		5a *because* I hear *that* you love all God's people
situation₂		5b and *that* you *continue to* believe/trust in the Lord Jesus.
	orienter	6a *I pray to God*
	means₁	6b that *by means of* your *continuing to* believe *in the Lord Jesus*
	means₂	6c *and* by means of *your* realizing/knowing all the good things which God/Christ *has given* to us(inc)
REACTION₂	RESULT MEANS	6d *you* may act effectively as a partner *to all God's people*,
	purpose	6e in order that Christ *may be honored* by God's people.
REACTION₃		7a I have rejoiced greatly and have been greatly encouraged
	generic	7b because you have acted lovingly *toward God's people*;
situation	SPECIFIC	7c *specifically*, you, brother,* have encouraged God's people [SYN]

**Throughout the displays of Philemon, when 'you' is unmarked as to being singular or plural, it is *singular*.

See p. 32 for vv. 8–11.

INTENT AND PARAGRAPH PATTERN

Expressions such as 'I have much joy and encouragement' and 'I always thank my God' identify the paragraph as one of expressive intent, especially since these expressions occur in the main constituents of the paragraph. It would seem that prayer in this context may also be expressive. However, the *situation* calling for the prayer is implicit

PROMINENCE AND THEME

Since this paragraph has three conjoined NUCLEI at the highest level, one's first reaction would be that each of the NUCLEI should be represented in the theme statement. But as Beekman and Callow (1974:320) mention, "The event of praying in verse 4 is, however, subsidiary to 'I thank'. It is represented in the surface structure by a participle and two abstract nouns, and when ὅπως is used in verse 6 to introduce the contents of the prayer, no finite verb is used." Also, Paul's response of thankfulness and joy to Philemon's love comes both before and after the prayer; this is a way of marking prominence. The theme statement is based, then, on NUCLEI 1 and 3 and includes the most prominent reason for the thankfulness and joy, Philemon's love for the saints (signaled as prominent by its repetition). This theme feeds directly into vv. 8–9 especially, and 8–11 as a whole, with its opening of 'therefore' and 'because of love [i.e., Philemon's love especially] I appeal rather than command'.

Note that 'you have shown' in the theme statement expresses the fact that Philemon's love had been manifested through concrete acts of encouraging the hearts of God's people.

NOTES

4a always There is a question as to whether πάντοτε 'always' modifies the main verb, εὐχαριστῶ 'I thank', which precedes it, or the participial phrase that follows it, μνείαν σου ποιούμενος 'making mention of you'. In other epistles, Paul uses πάντοτε 'always' after εὐχαριστῶ 'I thank' (cf. 1 Cor. 1:4 and 2 Thess. 1:3 especially) to unambiguously modify that verb. But πάντοτε can occur clause initially. It may very well be occurring clause initially in Phil. 1:4 in a construction similar to the one here. In Rom. 1:9 Paul uses ἀδιαλείπτως 'unceasingly', which is an adverb close in meaning to πάντοτε, before μνείαν ὑμῶν ποιοῦμαι 'I make mention of you'. However, a comparison with 1 Thess. 1:2 makes it seem likely that πάντοτε 'always' in Phlm. 4 is to be taken as modifying εὐχαριστῶ 'I thank'. The majority of commentators and versions do take it as modifying εὐχαριστῶ.

my God (*or,* **God** *whom I worship*) The alternative 'God whom I worship' is given in the display text since in some languages the word for God cannot occur in a 'genitive' relationship such as 'my God', so the role relationship may have to be propositionalized. Basis for the propositionalization given here can be found in such passages as Acts 27:23 where Paul identifies his God as "the God whose I am and whom I worship/serve."

4b when I pray for you This construction in the Greek text may be in participial form because Paul wants to mention next the reasons for (or content of) the thanksgiving, and so he needs to slightly decrease the focus on 'making mention of you in my prayers' to make the proper connection between 'I thank' and the reasons for the thanksgiving. Participles are not used in SSA propositionalization, but the same type of thing can be handled by using a proposition in the role of circumstance, 'when I pray for you' or 'when I mention your *name* when I pray'.

you, *Philemon* 'Philemon' is added here to clearly indicate that Paul is now speaking directly to Philemon rather than to any of the others named earlier or to them as a whole.

5a-b *because* **I hear** *that* **you love all God's people and** *that* **you** *continue to* **believe/trust in the Lord Jesus**

Is there a chastic structure in this verse? In literal translations such as that of the RSV, "because I hear of your love and of the faith which you have toward the Lord Jesus and all the saints," this verse may appear to mean that Philemon's trust was not only in the Lord Jesus but also in all God's people. The following are various attempts by commentators at a solution to this problem of interpretation:

1. πίστις here means only 'loyalty': 'You love and are loyal to the Lord Jesus, and you love and are loyal to all God's people'.
2. πίστις here means 'faith' when 'the Lord Jesus' is its object and πρός is the preposition, but it means 'loyalty' when 'all God's people' is its object and εἰς is the preposition: 'You love and believe in the Lord Jesus, and you love and are loyal to all God's people'. (Note, however, that εἰς occurs in the New Testament with πίστις in contexts where the meaning is 'believe in' or 'faith in'. See, for instance, Acts 24:24 and Col. 2:5.)
3. 'Faith' here has only 'the Lord Jesus' as its object, and 'love' has only 'all God's people' as its object: 'You believe in the Lord Jesus, and you love all God's people'. This interpretation appeals to the phenomenon of chiasmus.

The chiasmus solution is followed in the propositionalization for the following reasons:

1. The thanksgiving and prayer unit of Colossians (1:3-12), written at the same time as Philemon, and also that of Ephesians (1:15-23), which was written about the same time, both have as the reason for the thanksgiving the addressees' faith in Christ Jesus/the Lord Jesus and love for all the saints, τὴν πίστιν ὑμῶν ἐν Χριστῷ Ἰησοῦ καὶ τὴν ἀγάπην ἣν ἔχετε εἰς πάντας τοὺς ἁγίους 'the faith of-you(pl) in Christ Jesus and the love which you-have for all the saints' (Col. 1:4). All the relationships are almost exactly the same as when the chiasmus theory is applied to Phlm. 5. This includes the fact that faith and love retain the same senses in all three epistles. If interpretation 1 or 2 were to be followed, at least one of the words would have to be understood in a different sense.
2. In the chiasmus approach there is no problem grammatically with the collocation of τὴν ἀγάπην 'love' with εἰς πάντας τοὺς ἁγίους 'for all the saints' since this collocation also occurs in Col. 1:4 and Eph. 1:15. Although ἐν 'in' occurs in the Colossians and Ephesians passages linking τὴν πίστιν 'faith' with Χριστῷ Ἰησοῦ 'Christ Jesus' while πρός links these constituents in the Philemon chiasmus approach, πρός does occur in 1 Thess. 1:8 linking πίστις 'faith' with τὸν θεόν 'God': ἡ πίστις ὑμῶν ἡ πρὸς τὸν θεόν 'the faith of-you(pl) which is toward God'.

Once a chiasmus approach is assumed here, the resulting meanings and relationships are simpler and more straightforward than allowed by other interpretations. They also appear to be more appropriate to the focus of the larger context. Although it is true that examples of chiasmus on the sentence level are rare in the New Testament, when there is a construction on any level consisting of four constituents in which the first two are coordinate and each of these two is only related (or more closely related) to one of the second two constituents, it is quite common for the second of the two coordinate constituents to be followed immediately by the constituent to which it relates (or to which it relates more closely), thus producing an ABB'A' chiastic construction. (Cf. Lk. 9:1 where the second gift relates more closely to the first purpose and see also 1 Cor. 1:24–25, Col. 3:11a and the Titus SSA, Banker 1987:26–28.) Also, constructions such as τῇ κατ' οἶκον σου ἐκκλησίᾳ 'the at house of-you church' (Phlm. 2) show that it is not out of place in Greek for outer, noncontiguous constituents to be more closely related to each other than they are to contiguous constituents.

God's people Following the Colossians SSA (John Callow 1983:27), τοὺς ἁγίους is not rendered as 'saints' in the display text since "the biblical meaning is not its primary English sense any longer." Instead 'God's people' is used since "'saint' is understood to mean 'set apart for and belonging to God'."

6a *I pray to God*

Note that 'I pray' does not occur in the Greek text at this point. However, a majority of commentators interpret the ὅπως construction (all of v. 6) as the content of a prayer for Philemon. The reasons for such an interpretation are:

1. Paul often begins the body of his epistle with an introductory unit that includes both thanksgiving and prayer for the recipient(s).
2. In Eph. 1:16b, Paul uses an almost identical construction (μνείαν ποιούμενος ἐπὶ τῶν προσευχῶν μου 'making mention in my prayers') to the one he uses in Phlm. 4b to definitely act as the orienter for the following ἵνα construction that forms the content of the prayer.
3. The conjunction ὅπως often occurs after verbs of asking or praying to introduce the content of the petition or prayer.

Because the ὅπως construction is separated from what might be taken as its orienter ('making mention of you in my prayers') by the reasons for the thanksgiving (v. 5), a few commentators understand the ὅπως construction to depend upon τὴν πίστιν ἣν ἔχεις 'faith which you have' in v. 5, which is the nearest verbal construction to ὅπως.

Note that 'to God' is added after 'I pray' since in many languages it is necessary to state to whom one is praying. It may be in some languages, however, that 'God' will actually need to be explicitly stated as the one who causes or grants the request. For an example of how this may be done, see the alternate propositionalization at the end of the notes on this verse.

The structure of verse 6 The ὅπως construction (all of v. 6, the content of the prayer) is potentially the most difficult construction in the whole epistle to analyze, since there are many possible interpretations not only of the verse as a whole but of the various segments of the verse. In a prayer, the petitions are unrealized actions that are requested to be realized (or actions that are partially realized but are requested to be realized more and more). These petitions may be coordinate or supportive of one another. In this prayer, there is only one verb in the Greek text, γένηται 'may be', which occurs with ἐνεργής 'active, effective'. The sense, then, of this phrase is 'may be active, may be effective'. The fact that there is only one verbal form suggests that if there is more than one petition, the petitions of the prayer are not in coordinate relationship. The fact that there are prepositional phrases and genitive constructions with abstract nouns suggests that there very well may be other petitions in a supportive relationship with the petition represented by the verb. Since the petitions are unrealized but are to be realized, the supportive relationship will be means-purpose; and since they are *all* unrealized, the prominence will not necessarily be on the first means. It would seem best to consider the construction in which the only verb occurs as the most prominent in the chain, unless for some other reason this would seem inappropriate.

The grammatical head of the noun phrase which acts as subject of ἐνεργὴς γένηται 'may be effective' is ἡ κοινωνία 'the fellowship, the sharing', a topic that is very important to the theme of the whole epistle. The cognate word κοινωνόν 'partner' occurs in the most prominent and focal verse of the epistle, v. 17, where Paul wants Philemon to extend the partnership that he and Philemon have to Onesimus. Therefore, both the grammatical and contextual signals suggest that the construction with the verb is prominent.

6b–d *by means of* your *continuing to* believe *in the Lord Jesus . . .* you *may act effectively as a* partner *to all God's people*

A genitive following κοινωνία (unless it is a personal pronoun) normally refers to what is shared in or participated in or to those with whom there is fellowship. There seems to be only one place in the New Testament (Phil. 2:1) where the genitive following κοινωνία could be understood as the means, reason, or grounds for the κοινωνία, and even that one is in doubt. It is mentioned, though, in a TEV footnote as an alternate translation and in the notes of the *NIV Study Bible* (Barker 1985). It is not that the genitive following κοινωνία cannot function as the means or reason but that it does not normally do so. In fact, in many genitive constructions where the abstract nouns are other than κοινωνία, means or reason is often the function of the genitive.

A number of commentators do take ἡ κοινωνία τῆς πίστεώς σου 'the fellowship of your faith' here in Phlm. 6 as a construction where 'the faith of you' is in some way the means or cause of 'the fellowship' or 'sharing'. Hendriksen (1964) would interpret it as "the sharing to which your faith gives rise" or the sharing "springing from your faith." Lightfoot (1879) mentions "springing from thy faith" in both the notes and the paraphrase.

The basic problem with interpreting 'your faith' as that in which the fellowship or sharing consists is that this means someone other than Philemon is the agent of the event referred to by κοινωνία. Someone else must share in his faith; there would be no point in saying that he shares in his own faith. Since the event referred to by κοινωνία is signaled in the Greek as the main event of v. 6 and since v. 6 is very likely the content of the prayer, it would seem strange that someone other than Philemon would be the main person(s) involved in the events to be realized through that prayer. 'I pray that our(exc) fellowship in/sharing of your faith may be effective' does not seem appropriate, nor does 'I pray that God's people's fellowship in your faith may be effective' seem appropriate either. (Of some of the translations which take the genitive this way, NEB tries to alleviate the problem by translating as "your fellowship... in our common faith," but it is doubtful that the Greek can be interpreted by such a switch in the pronouns. TEV's "our fellowship with you as believers" would be better based on 'the fellowship of our faith' rather than 'the fellowship of your(sg) faith', which is in the Greek text.)

RSV translates ἡ κοινωνία τῆς πίστεώς σου as "the sharing of your faith." It is difficult to know exactly what the translators intended to mean by this translation, but it should be noted that 'sharing of your faith' is not necessarily to be understood in the same way as 'sharing your faith' is today. The primary meaning of expressions in modern-day Christian usage in English such as 'sharing your faith' and 'sharing the gospel' have to do with the proclamation of the faith. This would be taking the genitive here as an objective genitive, which is possible. But 'the sharing', or 'communication', could also mean sharing with other believers of the results of one's faith, such as showing love and compassion and helping others materially or in whatever way help is needed. This would appear more appropriate in this context than evangelization and is the sense used in the display text rendering.

In summary, τῆς πίστεώς σου 'your(sg) faith' is interpreted in the propositionalization as a genitive referring to the means of the fellowship, since it seems more appropriate to the context. It is certainly not grammatically incorrect to interpret the genitive following κοινωνία as one that encodes *means*.

act ... as a partner *to all God's people* Κοινωνία has such meanings as 'fellowship, sharing, participation, partnership, close relationship, fellow-feeling'. As grammatical subject of ἐνεργὴς γένηται 'be/become effective/active', κοινωνία here must not be something that is just an emotional feeling but something that results in concrete benefits for others. No doubt Paul has Onesimus especially in mind; so, in this specific case, κοινωνία most likely means Philemon's treating of his runaway slave as a Christian brother and sharing with him not only material benefits but even more importantly spiritual benefits, including the spiritual freedom and brotherhood that are in Christ. There is a question as to whether the English word 'fellowship' is adequate enough to describe this. 'Share' might be better, but it is difficult to know what to state as the object of 'share' in the propositionalization, especially since it is very difficult to find an object that would be both appropriate to the context and also appropriate to SSA rules regarding abstract nouns. Thus 'act as a partner' has been used in the display text, a verbal form of 'partnership'. Even this solution is not a wholly acceptable one, since the concept of partner as such may not be found in all languages; but it may be the best we can do.

In some languages 'act as a partner' may require stating whom the partnership is with. For that reason 'all God's people' is added in parentheses in the display. In both 5 and 7, 'God's people' are explicitly stated as the beneficiaries of Philemon's acts of love, so it seems best to use 'God's people' as beneficiaries of his actions here also.

and by means of your realizing/knowing all the good things which God/Christ has given to us(inc) This ἐν construction (ἐν ἐπιγνώσει παντὸς ἀγαθοῦ τοῦ ἐν ἡμῖν 'in knowledge of every good thing which (is) in us') is taken by many commentators to indicate what is to be effectively realized from the sharing or fellowship. A number of other commentators and translators take it as a means construction. This latter interpretation is followed in the display text for the following reasons:

1. An ἐν construction often functions as means.
2. Some translations (e.g., TEV's "will bring about a deeper understanding" and RSV's "may promote the knowledge of") actually interpret 'know' as the major event in the sentence. While this is possible, ἐπιγνώσει 'knowledge' occurs in a prepositional phrase, and prepositional phrases are not the norm for communicating the most prominent information. Moreover, "knowledge of all the good that is ours" (RSV) does not seem to be nearly as appropriate to the context of the epistle as fellowship. But when this interpretation is followed, as it is in TEV and RSV, it is knowledge that is made prominent.
3. Knowledge as a means to being able to do God's will, whatever God's will may be in a specific situation (here, properly fellowshiping with others), is certainly as much in line with the teaching of the Scriptures as is knowledge being the result of other Christian activities, such as fellowship. In fact, it is rather difficult to follow the progression of thought in such translations as NIV, "I pray that you may be active in sharing your faith, so that you will have a full understanding of every good thing we have in Christ." RSV is similar to this but more literal, "I pray that the sharing of your faith may promote the knowledge of all the good that is ours in Christ." It is difficult to know just what is meant by this. A majority of commentators take `all the good that is in us' as the spiritual blessings that are ours as Christians. It is easier to see how a knowledge of all that Christ has done for us will make us more active in our sharing with others than vice versa.

which God/Christ has given to us(inc) Some Greek manuscripts have τοῦ ἐν ἡμῖν 'which (is) in us', while others have τοῦ ἐν ὑμῖν 'which (is) in you(pl)'. In the UBS text (1993) ἡμῖν 'us' occurs as a B reading, that is, considered to be almost certain; ἡμῖν 'us' also occurs in the Majority Text (Hodges and Farstad 1985). Some commentators say that ὑμῖν 'you' has better manuscript evidence but not as good internal evidence as ἡμῖν 'us'. The only original difference in the two words was the η and the υ. But by the early second century A.D., they had come to be pronounced similarly. That may have led to the confusion here. Since σου, a second person (singular) pronoun, is the only other expressed personal agent in the ὅπως construction, a scribe may have thought a second person pronoun was intended here also, rather than a first person pronoun, and thus would have chosen ὑμῖν rather than ἡμῖν. Commentators tend to prefer the ἡμῖν 'us' reading, though they may admit the good evidence for ὑμῖν 'you(pl)' from the manuscripts.

all the good things which God/Christ has given to us(inc) There are basically two interpretations of παντὸς ἀγαθοῦ τοῦ ἐν ἡμῖν 'every good (thing) which (is) in us':

1. Every spiritual blessing that is in us (i.e., which the Lord has given to us).
2. Every good deed that is in us (i.e., which we are able to do).

Because the choice of ἡμῖν 'us' over ὑμῖν 'you(pl)' is based partially on internal considerations (i.e., the context), one has to be careful in building an argument for interpretation 1 or 2 based on the use of one of the pronouns rather than the other so as not to argue circularly. However, the only other personal agent in the ὅπως construction is referred to by σου, a second person singular form, rather than ὑμῶν, a second person plural form.

It is true that in v. 14 τὸ ἀγαθόν σου 'the good of you(sg)/your(sg) good (thing)' means 'your good deed', but here in v. 6 ἀγαθου is not modified by σου 'you(sg)' but by τοῦ ἐν ἡμῖν/ὑμῖν 'which is in us/you(pl)', so there is no necessary connection between the two.

If Philemon is interpreted as the agent of the fellowship/sharing, then it is slightly more likely that παντὸς ἀγαθοῦ τοῦ ἐν ἡμῖν refers to 'every spiritual blessing' since we might expect that if 'every good deed' were meant then the pronoun would be σου 'your(sg)' or τοῦ ἐν σοί 'which (is) in you(sg)' to agree in number and person with Philemon as agent of the sharing. But the pronoun is either ἡμῖν, which is, in effect, here a first person plural inclusive pronoun, or ὑμῖν 'you(pl)'. Still, as far as ἡμῖν is concerned, the deeds could also be thought of as universal, 'every good deed that we(inc) are able to do'.

If ὑμῖν 'you(pl)' is considered as having better textual evidence, then more likely πάντος ἀγαθοῦ 'every good (thing)' refers to 'every good deed you(pl) can do', though one wonders why Paul would have changed from singular to plural in a small four-verse unit that has no other 'you(pl)' and is directed exclusively to Philemon.

Most commentators take παντὸς ἀγαθοῦ τοῦ ἐν ἡμῖν as having a meaning such as 'every (spiritual) blessing we (have received)'.

6e in order that Christ *may be honored by God's people* Although εἰς Χριστόν 'for/in Christ' occurs at the end of the sentence with a long ἐν prepositional construction between it and the verb γένηται 'be/become', many commentators take it as modifying the central verbal construction rather than the ἐν construction or any part of it.

There are two questions that need to be answered: Does εἰς Χριστόν mean 'for Christ' or 'in Christ'? With what is it to be connected?

Ellicott's (1865) answer to the first question is as follows: "'unto Christ Jesus', not merely 'in reference to Him', but with a closer adherence to the primary force of the preposition, 'for the work of', 'to the honor of'." He follows the sound exegetical and semantic principle of understanding the primary meaning of the word or phrase unless there are sufficient reasons for understanding a secondary meaning. There is no doubt that εἰς may be translated as 'in' in certain circumstances, but one wonders if ἐν Χριστῷ 'in Christ' is not a set phrase and thus not susceptible to innovation. The display text follows the interpretation that takes εἰς in its primary meaning.

In answer to the second of the preceding questions, if εἰς Χριστόν is taken to mean 'for (the glory of) Christ', then its meaning is broad enough that it easily collocates with what comes immediately before it or with the central verbal construction, 'may become effective'. However, it would tend to receive more prominence if it were related to the more prominent (nuclear) proposition, and so that is what is done in the display text. There is no reason why 'for (the glory of) Christ' should not receive this greater prominence. At least as many commentators take it this way as take it with 'all the good that is in us', though more versions take it with 'all the good that is in us'.

Following this interpretation, then, εἰς Χριστόν propositionalizes as a purpose construction, most likely functioning as motivational purpose. In the propositionalization an agent needs to be supplied for the action of honoring Christ. If we take the action of honoring to be done by words, then someone other than Philemon will be the agent. These other people will see Philemon's good works as a partner and glorify Christ. If we take the action of honoring to be done by actions, then Philemon will be the agent of honoring Christ. It is difficult to make a decision on this, but since others are the beneficiaries of Philemon's partnership, it may be better to see others as involved in honoring Christ on the basis of Philemon's actions, even as Paul is at the very moment thanking God for Philemon's loving deeds. These 'others' would probably be 'God's people' who are explicitly mentioned as the beneficiaries of Philemon's loving actions in vv. 5 and 7.

Translations similar to the SSA propositionalization Considering the many choices of interpretation there are in this verse at so many points, it is noteworthy that the semantic analysis used here results in a translation quite similar relationally to that of Hendriksen (1964): "(Praying) that the sharing to which your faith gives rise may be energetically stimulated for Christ by the clear recognition of all the good that is ours. . . ." Also, it is not so very different from Vincent's (1897) paraphrase: "praying that in your full knowledge of every spiritual blessing which we as Christians possess, your faith may prove itself for the glory of Christ in the communication of its fruits to others."

It may be useful to suggest an alternate propositionalization for v. 6, since, to mark the prominence of a purpose construction over its means in the propositionalization, we used a 'by means of' construction twice in v. 6. This type of construction may not be so easy to handle in some languages. The following is an alternate propositionalization: '*I pray* that *God will cause* you *to continue to* believe *firmly in the Lord Jesus and cause you to* know all the good things which *he has given* to us(inc) *in order that you* may act effectively as a partner *to all God's people*. As a result, *they will honor* Christ'.

7a I have rejoiced greatly and have been greatly encouraged

How does v. 7 connect with what has come before? Verse 7 is connected with an antecedent unit by means of γάρ, which is often translated as 'for'. The most common function of γάρ in the New Testament is to indicate reason or grounds, but one of its other functions is described as "expressing continuation or connection" (BAGD, p. 152, entry 4). So one question to be answered is, Which of these two functions is intended here? The other is, γάρ relates v. 7 with what antecedent unit?

Since Paul mentions Philemon's love for others in v. 5 as one of the reasons for his thankfulness to God and expands upon this love in v. 7, Philemon's love for others is both the reason for his thanking God and for his rejoicing and encouragement. Paul may have definitely in mind that he is not only thankful to God for Philemon's love and faith but he is also thankful to him for the joy and encouragement he has received from Philemon's love for others, especially in encouraging the saints. If this is the case, then γάρ is used in its primary function of reason and relates back to εὐχαριστῶ τῷ θεῷ μου 'I thank my God' in 4a.

Another possibility is that Paul is no longer focusing on 'I thank my God' per se as the result (or orienter) but is using another expression to describe his reaction to Philemon's love. In this case γάρ would signal the continuation of the same type of reasoning, the same semantic domain, as in 4a and 5. Paul's thankfulness to God in this thanksgiving and prayer section would be in the background in v. 7 but not in the direct line of reasoning.

It is difficult to know which of these two options Paul had in mind as he wrote this part of the epistle, but we have chosen to keep the simpler, shortened form (the second option), especially since there is no overriding reason why 'I thank my God' needs to be made explicit in v. 7. In fact, its addition almost seems to downplay the prominence and effect of 'I rejoice greatly and have been greatly encouraged'. However, Paul may have been thinking more in line with the first option, and so we also present an alternate propositionalization: '*I thank my God* because I have rejoiced greatly and have been greatly encouraged because you have acted lovingly *toward God's people*'.

Tense considerations in 7a Regarding ἔσχον, translated by RSV as "I have derived [much joy . . .]," the aorist aspect in ἔσχον is usually taken to refer to the event of gaining possession, 'I got/acquired', rather than the state of possessing, 'I had'. But here it need not be seen as referring to an isolated demonstration of love on Philemon's part that once brought joy to Paul. Rather, since Paul heard of his love on more than one occasion (as the present tense of ἀκούων 'hearing' in 5a would indicate), the implication seems to be that his proven character is in view. So it seems most likely that Paul's joy is seen as extending over a period from the past until the present. Some Greek exegetes make a point of the fact that the aorist ἔσχον here should be translated as 'had' and refers basically to the time of the hearing of the love. However, in most versions the tendency is to translate either with an aspect of the lasting effect of the joy and encouragement or at least with no necessary intimation that it was only something now past.

There is a similar situation with the aorist form ἐχάρην for 'rejoice' in Phil. 4:10. In some versions (RSV, NIV, TEV, for instance), this aorist is translated as a present tense in English. In fact, with ἤδη 'now' in the immediate context, it seems strange to translate otherwise. RSV has "I rejoice in the Lord greatly that now at length you have revived your concern for me." It would appear that, both in Phil. 4:10 and Phlm. 7, tense function does not correspond between English and Greek, and so different tenses need to be used, tenses that do not imply that the rejoicing is a thing of the past. So, 'I have rejoiced greatly and have been greatly encouraged' is used in the display text.

I . . . have been greatly encouraged The display text presents 'encouraged' here as a state rather than an action, and so Philemon has not been supplied as the agent of the action of encouraging Paul. Of course, if in any language this needs to be stated as an action, Philemon would be the agent: '*You* have caused me to be very happy and have greatly encouraged me because you have acted lovingly *toward God's people*. . . .'

7b because you have acted lovingly *toward God's people* The ἐπί here, in ἐπὶ τῇ ἀγάπῃ σου 'from your love', is listed in BAGD, p. 152, under entry II.1.b, "of that upon which a state of being, an action, or a result is based." It is clear that Paul's joy and encouragement are the results of Philemon's love. In this context, 'love', of course, refers to acts of love, the measure of all true love. Based on the generic-specific relationship adopted in the following note, the beneficiaries of that love are God's people. They are the explicit beneficiaries of the refreshing, or encouragement, in 7c and also of Philemon's love in 5.

7c *specifically,* **you, brother,* have encouraged God's people**

The relationship between 7b and 7c Following the Beekman-Callow analysis (1974: 364), these two successive reason constructions are interpreted as being in a generic-specific relationship with each other. 'I have rejoiced greatly and have been greatly encouraged' is the result to which they both relate. Paul rejoiced because Philemon acted lovingly; specifically, he cheered the hearts of God's people. It would appear that one of the functions of τῇ ἀγάπῃ σου 'your(sg) love' is to act as a link to σου τὴν ἀγάπην 'your(sg) love' in v. 5; the ὅτι construction then expands on this, being more specific.

There are indications that 7c, the specific proposition, is more prominent than its generic counterpart, 7b. When there is only one specific, it is often signaled in some way as more prominent than its generic counterpart. Here Paul's use of the vocative ἀδελφέ 'brother' after the σου 'you(sg)' in the specific unit instead of after the σου in the generic unit suggests that he is giving more prominence to the specific unit.

have encouraged God's people The word 'heart' (in 'the hearts of the saints') is an example of synecdoche. It stands for the whole person; and since it does not act as a live figure of speech here, it is translated by its nonfigurative meaning in the display text. (Of course, in a language where 'heart' has generally the same sense and function as 'heart' has in Greek in this context, using 'the hearts of God's people' *may* be more communicative of the original message than using 'God's people' alone.)

Either 'have been encouraged' or 'have been cheered' would be an appropriate translation of ἀναπέπαυται in this context. In the display text the active form is used rather than the passive.

brother* Again, 'brother' is asterisked here because it does not have its primary English meaning of a biological brother but of a Christian brother. The Greek text has only ἀδελφέ 'brother' and not ἀδελφέ μου 'my brother'. In many languages the vocative may occur only in the initial position in the paragraph or sentence and never finally as here in the Greek text at the very end of v. 7. In fact, it may be that in some languages the vocative occurs only discourse initially to address the audience at the beginning of the discourse. It is quite apparent that at least one of its functions here is to signal the prominence of the clause it follows. And here it would appear that its placement right after διὰ σοῦ 'through you(sg)' puts special emphasis on Philemon as agent of these good works of encouraging God's people. Another function of the vocative here might be that of signaling the rapport inherent in the word 'brother' itself, and since the content of the clause deals with a rapport relationship anyway, these two functions would work together to double the effect here.

These same functions are operative in English also, and it seems best in English to place 'brother' after 'you' (functioning as agent) in the display text: 'you, brother,* have encouraged God's people'; or alternatively, this could be propositionalized as 'God's people have been encouraged by you, brother*'. In languages in which the vocative does not have these functions, it may be best to leave the vocative out altogether, especially if its inclusion sounds unnatural. For those languages in which at least some of the effect of these functions is carried by the vocative but the vocative must occur at the beginning of the sentence, it may be placed there if the overall rapport of the sentence is thereby strengthened.

SECTION CONSTITUENT 8–11 (Paragraph: Inference of 4–7)

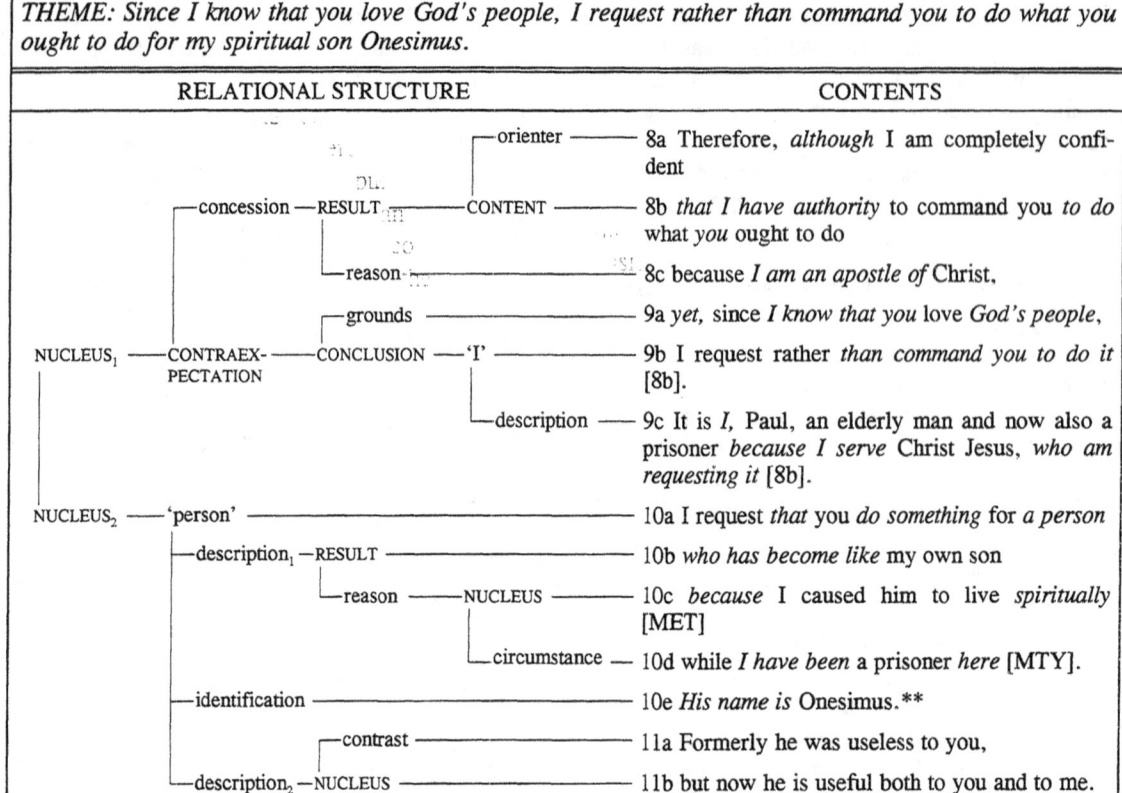

PROMINENCE AND THEME

There are two constituents in this paragraph which the display diagram shows as naturally prominent—9b and 10a. However, in the Greek text, 10b would also be a part of the second naturally prominent construction; in the propositionalization and diagramming, it has necessarily been separated from 10a for various reasons. Also, though in the Greek text 'Onesimus' as a name is not introduced in the naturally prominent constituents but introduced later on, there is ample reason for including it in the theme since his identification is extremely important to the letter and, in fact, the unexpected delay in revealing his name is in itself a feature of prominence.

Since in this whole section Paul has made Philemon's love for others the main basis for his decision to request rather than command, it is appropriate to include 9a in the theme also. We would expect grounds to be included in the theme along with the conclusion anyway.

NOTES

8a although The occurrence of μᾶλλον 'rather' in v. 9 shows that the Greek participial phrase that forms v. 8 is concessive.

I am completely confident Depending upon the context, παρρησία may have either the sense of 'confidence' or 'boldness'. An example of the first is in 2 Cor. 7:4, which the NIV renders, "I have great confidence in you." The question is, With which sense, 'confidence' or 'boldness', is παρρησία used in Philemon 8?

The word 'command' shows that authority is in focus here. In English, boldness in connection with authority may mean (1) doing what one does not have the authority to do, or (2) doing what one *believes* he has the authority to do but others may not, or (3) doing what one has the authority to do but would not be expected to do. Of these three kinds of 'boldness', the first would definitely not be pertinent here and the second, in all likelihood, would not be pertinent since Paul is speaking from his own perspective. The third sense, then, would be the only possibility, in which case Paul may have been politely referring to his use of authority. Following this interpretation NEB has, "although in Christ I might make bold to point out your duty."

However, it would almost seem that the use of 'boldness' in some English translations is either a strict literal translation of what is believed to be the primary lexical meaning of παρρησία without reference to the context, or a development of that meaning in the context according to *English* senses of 'boldness' rather than according to Greek. For, in fact, the straightforward meaning of the Greek παρρησία is 'confidence' here.

Erdman (1933) says, "By 'all boldness' Paul means 'ample ground for a claim.'" In other words, Paul is saying that he has ample authority in Christ to command Philemon to do what should be done.

8b what *you* ought to do The phrase 'what *you* ought to do' refers, of course, to the proper reception and treatment of Onesimus; in other words, it is a reference to the content of the major *APPEAL*. According to BAGD, p. 66, entry 2, the meaning of τὸ ἀνῆκον is 'what is proper, one's duty', and this has been rendered in the display text as 'what *you* ought to do'.

8c because *I am an apostle of* Christ, Paul is referring to his authority as a Christian apostle and not merely as a Christian brother when he uses 'in Christ', since Scripture does not suggest that Christians have authority over other Christians unless they have a position in the church.

As to the relationship of 8c, the display diagram shows that 'because *I am an apostle of Christ*' applies to all of 8a-b and not to the relative clause 'what *you* ought to do'.

9a yet, since *I know that you* love *God's people* The word διά, translated by RSV as "for the sake of," is also commonly used to express reason, so NIV's "on the basis of love" is just as valid a translation on a lexical basis.

The major problem here is determining the agent and beneficiary of this love since there is no noun or pronoun indicating agent or beneficiary, as there is in vv. 5 and 7. There is, of course, no such thing as love without someone loving or being loved. A number of commentators understand this love as a general Christian love—the love which Christians do have, or should have, for one another. A few commentators understand Paul as the agent and Philemon as the goal of the love, probably because Paul is the agent of the main verb of the clause, παρακαλῶ 'I appeal'. There is some very good evidence, however, that τὴν ἀγάπην ('love' preceded by the article) refers to Philemon's love for God's people mentioned in 4–7. Very often the article with abstract nouns is anaphoric, and a back-reference to 7 is very suitable here. The phrase διὰ τὴν ἀγάπην, then, resumes and explains διό 'therefore' after the intervening concession. Contextually the known character of Philemon seems the most suitable grounds for proceeding with the appeal. This interpretation is the basis for the display text reading.

However, if τὴν ἀγάπην is not understood as only an anaphoric reference to Philemon's love for God's people, the best way to propositionalize διὰ τὴν ἀγάπην 'because of love' appears to be: 'since *I know that you* love *all God's people* and since *I* love *you*'.

The inclusion of Philemon's love for all God's people avoids the downplay of this important part of the argument. It implicitly includes Philemon's love for Paul, a relationship that probably does not need to be mentioned more explicitly, however. It also includes Paul's love for Philemon, which makes sense in this context and may be what Paul intended to include, since as agent of the main verb and of the sentence in general, it is quite natural that he would be agent of the love (that is, if we do not understand τὴν ἀγάπην as only anaphoric to Philemon's love for the saints as stated in 4–7).

Note that in the propositionalization adopted in the display text, the logical reasoning is clearer if Paul's *knowledge* of Philemon's love for God's people is made explicit: 'since *I know that you* love *God's people*, I request rather *than command you to do it*'.

9b request In BAGD, p. 617, the occurrences of παρακαλῶ in vv. 9 and 10 are listed under entry 3, "*request, implore, appeal to, entreat,*" rather than under entry 2, "*appeal to, urge, exhort, encourage.*" If μᾶλλον 'rather' and the whole concessive clause in 8 are to mean anything, the meaning of παρακαλῶ here cannot be the same as 'command', which the sense 'exhort/urge' might almost suggest, especially as it is used in some contexts in Scripture. (See 2 Thess. 3:12 where παραγγέλλομεν 'we command' and παρακαλοῦμεν 'we urge' are treated basically as synonyms.) On the other hand, one would not want to use a word that implies that Paul is *begging* Philemon to do something for him.

9c I, Paul, an elderly man . . . Rather than the connection expressed in this propositionalization and in KJV ("being such an one as Paul the aged . . ."), some commentators take τοιοῦτος ὤν 'being such a one' as the end of a sentence, and they give it a meaning, as, for example, Meyer (1885) did: "Since such is my manner of thinking and dealing, that, namely, in place of commanding thee, I rather for love's sake betake myself to the παρακαλεῖν ['appeal']." Greek exegetes are divided in their opinion. Some maintain that ὡς 'as' never occurs with τοιοῦτος 'such a one', with the implication that translations such as KJV are not based on good Greek analysis. Lightfoot, however, presents what would seem to be good examples from ancient Greek secular writers of forms of τοιοῦτος occurring with ὥσπερ '(just) as' and also states that early biblical commentators who wrote in Greek "without a single exception connect the words τοιοῦτος ὤν ὡς Παῦλος together." As mentioned, the display text rendering is based on this latter interpretation that τοιοῦτος ὤν 'being such a one' is connected with ὡς Παῦλος . . . 'as Paul . . .'; note, however, that if the other interpretation is followed, then the love referred to in 9a would be Paul's love.

an elderly man and now also a prisoner *because I serve* **Christ Jesus** A very important question here is whether πρεσβύτης 'elderly man/ambassador' and δέσμιος Χριστοῦ Ἰησοῦ 'prisoner of Christ Jesus' are words designating authority and are thus concessive to Paul's decision to request rather than command, or they are words appealing to Philemon's sense of compassion and respect and thus form a motivation for fulfilling the content of the request. We might say that if πρεσβύτης means 'ambassador', then the idea will be concessive, but if it means 'elderly man', it will indicate motivation. At the same time, *both* πρεσβύτης and δέσμιος Χριστοῦ Ἰησοῦ will indicate either concession or motivation; in this construction, the one can hardly indicate concession and the other motivation.

The form πρεσβύτης in the Greek text of Philemon 9 is the basic form for 'old man', while πρεσβευτής is the basic form for 'ambassador'. However, πρεσβύτης can also be an alternate spelling for πρεσβευτής 'ambassador'. Those who find 'old man' difficult understand πρεσβύτης as an alternate spelling for πρεσβευτής 'ambassador'. But where Paul uses the ambassador metaphor elsewhere, it is in the context of evangelism (2 Cor. 5:20; Eph. 6:20); and it is not appropriate in the Philemon epistle. Paul is not focusing here on his imprisonment as a means of evangelism. Nor in 2 Cor. 5:20 and Eph. 6:20 is he focusing on an ambassador's authoritative position. It is difficult to come to any conclusion on this on the basis of orthography; but it seems a little strange to appeal to the use of 'ambassador' as an authoritative position when it is not used as such elsewhere in the epistles. Also, it seems somewhat strained to say that, since Philemon's son Archippus was old enough to be called Paul's fellow soldier, Paul would not call himself an old man in relation to Philemon. It is, after all, only conjecture that Archippus was Philemon's son. Moreover, "according to Hippocrates, a man was called πρεσβύτης from forty-nine to fifty-six; after that, γέρων" (Vincent 1897).

It is also difficult to prove that Paul uses δέσμιος Χριστοῦ Ἰησοῦ 'prisoner of Christ Jesus' as a title of authority. Nowhere else in the New Testament can δέσμιος or its cognates definitely be shown to have this sense. In Eph. 4:1 Paul uses ὁ δέσμιος ἐν κυρίῳ 'a prisoner in the Lord' in combination with παρακαλῶ 'I appeal/urge': "I therefore, a prisoner for the Lord, beg you . . ." (RSV). But this is not a statement of authority—it is a request for respect. Here in v. 9 δέσμιος Χριστοῦ Ἰησοῦ is best interpreted as in v. 1a. As Lightfoot says in his comments on Phlm. 1, "The authoritative title of 'Apostle' is dropped, because throughout this letter St. Paul desires to entreat rather than to command (ver. 8, 9). . . . In its place is substituted a designation which would touch his friend's heart. How could Philemon resist an appeal which was penned within prison walls and by a manacled hand?" It would seem very reasonable that Paul would start out at the very beginning of the letter with the nonauthoritarian tone in which the whole letter is written. It is therefore difficult to see how δέσμιος Χριστοῦ Ἰησοῦ 'prisoner of Christ Jesus' could become a title of authority by v. 9, as Lightfoot also maintains.

now also a prisoner *because I serve* **Christ Jesus** Whereas 'a prisoner *who serves* Christ Jesus' seems more appropriate as a translation of δέσμιος Χριστοῦ Ἰησοῦ 'prisoner of Christ Jesus' in v. 1, 'a prisoner *because I serve* Christ Jesus' seems more appropriate here since the reason for his imprisonment seems more in focus here than a basic statement of the relationship. It is not only the fact of his being a prisoner but also the fact that he is a prisoner because he serves Christ that should motivate Philemon to agree to Paul's request. The explicit stating of the reason for his imprisonment makes this clear.

now Both here and in 11b, the Greek word νῦν is made more emphatic by the addition of the demonstrative suffix ι: νυνί 'now'.

The relationship of 9b and 10a, the two main propositions that contain 'I appeal' In earlier SSA-type work on Philemon, it was suggested that 9b and 10a have a contraction-NUCLEUS relationship, since they both contain the major verb of the paragraph, παρακαλῶ 'I appeal', and the second occurrence appears to govern the basic substance of the appeal as far as this paragraph is concerned. But these two constituents are actually dealing with two different aspects of the appeal. In 9b it is stated that Paul would rather appeal than command, while in 10 the topic of the appeal, Onesimus, is stated and described. Thus it would seem better to label 9b and 10a as separate nuclei.

The function of 9c On the propositional level, 9c is a description of Paul, the agent of the appeal. But its purpose is to function as motivation, not for making the appeal but for Philemon to respond to the appeal. Paul does not make the appeal because he is an elderly man and a prisoner of Christ Jesus; he makes the appeal because he wants Philemon to do the right thing for Onesimus in this case. Also, Paul does not request rather than command because he is an elderly man and a prisoner of Christ Jesus but because he believes that in the case of Philemon, a man who is growing into real love for others, this is the best thing to do. Paul describes himself in these terms because he believes such a description will aid in his overall purpose of encouraging Philemon to have the right attitude and thus be willing to grant Paul's request of welcoming Onesimus back in the right way. The descriptions in vv. 10–11 have the same function.

10c *because* I caused him to live *spiritually* 'Whom I have begotten' is a live metaphor since 'child' also occurs in the context, belonging to the same, larger figure. It should be noted that English translations such as 'whose father I have become' which seek for a contemporary equivalent of ἐγέννησα 'I have begotten', while being more natural English, tend to downplay (unintentionally) the initiative of the father, which in this case is probably significant.

The implied point of similarity is the process through which one person brings life to another. Just as a father causes physical life to come to his offspring, so Paul caused spiritual life to come to Onesimus (cf. 1 Cor. 4:15). Of course, the Holy Spirit is the source of spiritual life, just as he is the source of physical life; but here it is the means, not the source, that is in focus. So in order to maintain proper focus *in this context*, the source is not included in the display text, even as it is not included in the original text.

For languages that need to spell out the metaphor in detail, the following propositionalization would be more appropriate: '*because* I caused him to live *spiritually just as someone's father causes his son to live physically*'. A rendering that would describe the same experience but would be easier to translate in some languages would be, '*because* I caused/helped/led him to believe in Christ'.

10d while *I have been* a prisoner *here* A literal rendering of ἐν τοῖς δεσμοῖς is 'in the/these bonds'. But this Greek word for bonds is often used as a metonymy for 'imprisonment, custody'. Here it is rendered in the display text as 'while *I have been* a prisoner *here*'. It might also be rendered as 'while *I have been* in prison *here*'. But note that it is difficult to know whether Paul was confined in an actual prison or not, and whether he was chained or not. (In Acts 28, for instance, he was confined in a private home and chained, presumably, to a guard.)

10e–11b *His name is* Onesimus It is important to note that the identification is deliberately withheld until after the description of the man as Paul's convert. In the Greek text (as in the display text), the name Onesimus occurs only at the very end of v. 10. This is, no doubt, because Paul does not want to cause a negative reaction in Philemon's mind too early in his argument. He wants to prepare Philemon's mind as much as possible before he has to mention the topic of his request, Onesimus. He hs now come to the point where he must identify him.

Onesimus. Formerly he was useless to you, but now he is useful both to you and to me Ὀνήσιμος means 'useful, profitable, helpful', and so there is a play on words here. (In the Greek text the words for 'useless' and 'useful' are from a different root than the one for Onesimus.) Although most commentators do not deal with the function of the word play, Erdman (1933) says, "Well did Paul anticipate the reaction which the name would produce in the mind of Philemon—the name of a worthless, criminal, Phrygian slave. Thus at once he diverts the thought and counteracts the effect by an affectionate play upon the name. 'Onesimus, did I say? Onesimus means "helpful," "gainful." Full well do I know that he once was unprofitable to thee, but now is profitable to thee and me'."

Of course, it is very difficult to keep the word play in translating into other languages. The best that can be done in most languages is to transliterate the name and have a footnote to explain that Onesimus means 'useful' in Greek. This is what is done in the display text. An alternative would be, '*His name is* Onesimus, *which as you know means "useful"*'.

Formerly he was useless to you Certainly this refers to his running away, and it may possibly also describe his character before he ran away.

useful both to you and to me Paul indicates in v. 13 that Onesimus would be helpful to him in meeting his needs in prison. This probably indicates that Onesimus had already done this to some extent, though probably not for very long since Paul did not feel right about keeping someone else's slave. (See notes on vv. 13 and 14.) On the basis of Onesimus' present service which results from his Christian commitment, Paul can state that Onesimus will be useful to Philemon.

DIVISION CONSTITUENT 12-21 (Section: Nucleus of the body)

THEME: Onesimus is as dear to me as my own self (and should now be even dearer to you than he is to me); therefore, please receive him as you would receive me. I will repay to you whatever he owes you.

MACROSTRUCTURE	CONTENTS
basis₁	12-16 I am sending Onesimus back to you. He is as dear to me as my own self, and he will now be even dearer to you than he is to me.
APPEAL	17 Therefore, if you consider me your partner, receive him as you would receive me.
basis₂	18-19 I guarantee to repay to you whatever he owes you.
basis₃	20 Please encourage me in this matter as you encourage other believers in Christ.
basis₄	21 I have written this letter to you confident of your compliance with my request.

See p. 40 for vv. 12-16; p. 46 for v. 17; p. 48 for vv. 18-19; p. 52 for v. 20; p. 55 for v. 21.

STRUCTURE AND BOUNDARIES

For the initial boundary see division constituent 4-11.

Division constituent 12-21 forms a typical hortatory unit made up of *basis* and APPEAL constituents. Note that this is a paragraph pattern functioning on a higher level than the paragraph. A typical *basis* unit is formed by 12-16 with clear support for the major APPEAL in 17b, the οὖν in 17a signaling this. However, there are problems in the verses following 17b in distinguishing *basis* from other roles.

There are three imperatives in this section: προσλαβοῦ 'receive' ('receive him as me' in 17b); ἐλλόγα 'charge' ('charge that to me' in 18c); ἀνάπαυσον 'refresh' ('refresh my heart in Christ' in 20b). And there is an optative, ὀναίμην 'may I have benefit' ('may I have benefit from you in the Lord' in 20a). However, only the προσλαβοῦ 'receive' construction functions as the APPEAL in this hortatory unit. The other imperatives occur in motivational-type *basis* units. Verses 18-19 fit the commonly used Greek method of *refutation* in which the author or speaker answers already known or suspected objections to his appeal. The purpose of such a unit is to motivate the addressee to carry out the appeal by showing him that his objections are not valid.

The optative and imperative constructions in 20 fit another typical constituent of ancient rhetoric, *the appeal to the emotions*. This again is motivational, its purpose being to appeal to Philemon on the emotional level so that he will carry out the injunction in 17b.

Verse 21 appears to function both as motivational *basis* for carrying out the major APPEAL (17b) and as a closure of the hortatory section of the epistle. By expressing confidence in Philemon's compliance with his request, he encourages Philemon to accept Onesimus properly and retains rapport with Philemon, not wanting, of course, to close the argument on a negative note.

But what is the function of v. 22 and where does it belong? Verse 21 is the last verse that clearly refers to the APPEAL in 17b to receive Onesimus back properly. 'Your compliance' and 'you will do more than I say' definitely refer to the same general event as 'receive him as me'. 'Prepare a guest room for me' refers to a completely different event, and some commentators see this verse as dealing only with a completely different matter and only coincidental with the receiving of Onesimus, the primary matter of the epistle.

There are good reasons, however, for understanding v. 22 to have some connection with the major APPEAL of 17b. No definite time is given as to when Paul will be coming. He does not state the details of his situation so that Philemon might have some definite idea of when he might come. So it would seem that Paul is not setting up a definite appointment or schedule. In faith he expects that his coming will be soon, but he cannot say when that coming will be.

If ἑτοίμαζέ μοι ξενίαν 'prepare a guest room for me' is understood as not just a coincidental announcement of his proposed coming, then it will be seen that this request is similar in some respects to the request in 17b. Vincent (1897) in his paraphrase translates, "While you thus receive Onesimus, be ready to receive me also, and prepare a lodging for me. . . ." Paul also would like to be coming now to visit Philemon, but he cannot, so he asks Philemon to be prepared to receive him when he can come: 'Welcome Onesimus now, be ready to welcome me in the future (as soon as I can get there)'. So both APPEALS (17b and 22a) deal with receiving someone and giving him hospitality. This APPEAL in 22a, then, can be seen as a desire by Paul to keep Philemon, Onesimus, and himself in a close-knit group, something he has been endeavoring to do throughout the epistle (especially in vv. 16 and 17, but elsewhere also).

Paul is seeking to maintain good rapport between Philemon and himself, for he knows that this will motivate Philemon to receive Onesimus in a proper Christian way. Verse 22 is less directly motivational than 12-21 and would appear to have a role of closing rapport (even as the *introduction*, 8-11, has a function of opening rapport) and would be on the body level. This unit might be called *closure*. Paul is announcing his coming, but he is doing so in the context of the whole body of the letter and not as a totally separate item of business.

PROMINENCE AND THEME

In a hortatory unit theme, it is appropriate to include not only the APPEAL but also at least some representation of the *basis* for the APPEAL. There are two types of *basis* here. One is the more logical, reasoning type (12-16, 18-19); the other is more purely motivational (20, 21). The second type is not so focal to the basic argument so is not included in the theme, except that 'please' might help to represent the emotional appeal of 20. The major argument is 12-16, but the theme of 18-19 is included since the only reason for excluding 18-19 (the refutation of objections to the APPEAL) would be for the sake of brevity.

Although 17a is also considered basis, or grounds, for the APPEAL of 17b, it is not represented in the theme. It is more of a reminder of something that Philemon presumably took for granted than new information he should know in order to make the right decision, though it is true that this reminder is a key premise in the argument.

THE ARGUMENT OF 12-17

There appear to be two arguments developed by Paul in 12-17. The first: 'I cannot keep Onesimus here without your consent, and perhaps Onesimus was separated from you for a little while in order that you would have him back forever as a dear brother in the Lord; therefore, I am sending him back to you; therefore, receive him (as a dear brother in the Lord)'.

The second: the description of Onesimus right in the prominent opening verse of this paragraph as 'my very own heart' (τὰ ἐμὰ σπλάγχνα) is meant as the basis for Paul's APPEAL 'receive him as me'. This second argument is based on a combination of the following syllogisms:

1. Partners receive one another graciously (major premise); you consider me your partner (minor premise); therefore, you will receive me graciously (conclusion).
2. People who are as dear to each other as their own hearts should be treated in the same way (major premise); Onesimus is as dear to me as my own heart (minor premise); therefore, you should treat Onesimus as you would treat me (conclusion).

The major premise of 2 might be more appropriately stated as 'people who are as dear to each other as their own hearts should be treated by their (other) partners in the same way'.

Verse 17a, 'if you consider me your partner', is a reminder to Philemon that the minor premise of 1 is (or should be?) true. Verse 17b, 'receive him as you would receive me', is a combination of the two conclusions.

The first of the two arguments set forth here is encoded in the more basic part of the relational structure, deals with the basic events of sending and receiving, and is less motivational. Note that situationally it is made clear that Paul had no other choice than to send Onesimus back and that Philemon did not have to be persuaded to receive him. It was the manner of reception that needed persuasion. However, even though there is no explicit grammatical marker of reason at the beginning of 13, the other grammatical and semantic signals in 12-14 quite clearly indicate that 13-14 functions as a reason for sending Onesimus back. And γάρ at the beginning of 15 is a marker that more often than not signals reason. An alternate analysis, however, would be that 15-16 is not a second reason for sending Onesimus back but a conjoined (coordinate) unit to 12–14, a unit that deals with the motivational idea of Onesimus now being a dear brother in the Lord. Sometimes γάρ, when it does not signal a direct result-reason relationship, signals a further point in the general reasoning or discussion of a unit. Also, a point could be made that v. 15, 'Perhaps he was separated from you for a little while in order that you would have him back forever as a dear brother', functions better as an independent thought than one that needs to be connected back to 'I am sending him back'.

Since the argument that is more closely related to the basic relational structure (argument one) is less motivational (and therefore less supportive of the APPEAL in 17) than the other argument, and since taking γάρ as signaling a direct result-reason relationship is not wholly satisfactory, it is probably better not to add '*I am sending him back* because' at the beginning of 13 or 15 in the propositionalization or in most translations.

Note that, although vv. 15–16 come right before the APPEAL and Paul uses intensive language to persuade Philemon that Onesimus will now be a dear brother in the Lord and therefore should be received as such, he does not explicitly make reference to these factors in the APPEAL of 17 itself. In fact, it may be that because these factors have just been mentioned, he does not have to refer to them again. They certainly are implicit in the APPEAL, 'receive him as you would receive me'.

SECTION CONSTITUENT 12–16 (Paragraph: Basis₁ for the appeal of 17)

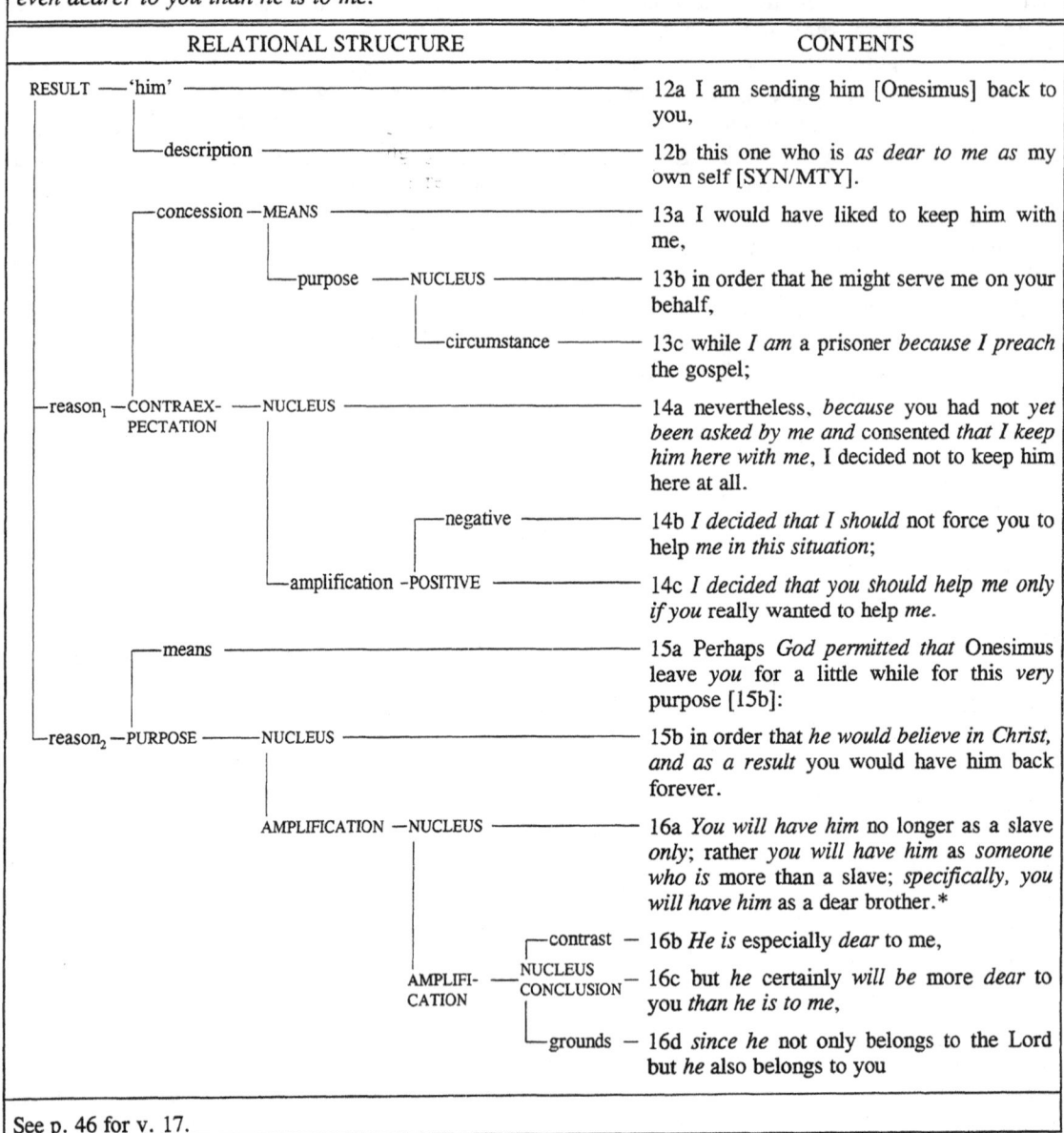

See p. 46 for v. 17.

BOUNDARIES AND COHERENCE

In a hortatory unit, when there is a definite break grammatically at the point where a long succession of indicative verbs (i.e., indicating basis) gives way to an imperative, as happens in 17, there is a good chance that a new paragraph is intended by the author. The οὖν 'therefore' at the beginning of 17 also indicates the break from *basis* to APPEAL. In fact, it is the most likely grammatical marker of a new paragraph in all of 8–20.

Note the following coherence factors within 12–16:

1. A series of non-imperative verbs that deal with Onesimus' movement or location: ἀνέπεμψα 'send back', κατέχειν 'keep', ἐχωρίσθη 'go away, be taken away', ἀπέχῃς 'have back'.

2. Rhetorical bracketing with reference to the dearness of Onesimus to Paul and Philemon: τὰ ἐμὰ σπλάγχνα 'my own heart' (v. 12); and ἀδελφὸν ἀγαπητόν, μάλιστα ἐμοί, πόσῳ δὲ

μᾶλλον σοὶ καὶ ἐν σαρκὶ καὶ ἐν κυρίῳ 'a dear brother, especially to me, but how much more to you, both in the flesh and in the Lord' (v. 16).

Affection is hinted at in v. 10 in τοῦ ἐμοῦ τέκνου 'my own child', but this might be seen as more of a tail-head link at the end of the introductory paragraph of 8-11.

PROMINENCE AND THEME

The presence of the same relative pronoun at the beginning of both v. 12 and v. 13 makes it more difficult to interpret Greek natural prominence signals than is often the case. But there seems little doubt that ὃν ἀνέπεμψά σοι 'whom I have sent back to you' is the most prominent core for 12-14, whether 13-14 be taken as reason for, or amplification of, 12. But in this *basis* unit, the sending back itself corresponds only to προσλαβοῦ 'receive' of the APPEAL. What Paul is most concerned with is the manner of that reception. Both the syntax and the content of the rest of 12 signal that 12b is being marked as prominent (see notes on that verse). Paul wants to make a point of the fact that Onesimus is to him as his own heart so that he can say in the APPEAL in 17, 'Receive him as me'. Verse 13 goes on to elaborate on how much Onesimus means to him, while 14 shows that nonetheless he must send him back, thus supporting 12a.

In 15, Paul begins a second, though related, line of reasoning. It is difficult to see why Paul would need to convince Philemon that he was right in sending Onesimus back. What he needs to convince Philemon about is the manner of the reception. We find in 15 that the ἵνα purpose construction is marked prominent by the use of διὰ τοῦτο 'for this purpose' and that the purpose construction extends to the end of 16. The point that Paul is trying to make is not only that Philemon will have Onesimus back forever but that he will have him back forever as a dear Christian brother, even dearer than he is to Paul. The *basis* unit thus ends as it started, showing that Onesimus is a dear brother, not only to Paul but also to Philemon himself. This rhetorical bracketing structure is not only a signal of coherence but also of prominence. Thus the theme is interpreted to be: 'I am sending Onesimus back to you. He is as dear to me as my own self, and he will now be even dearer to you than he is to me'.

NOTES

12 The Greek text The Greek text of this verse has variations in the manuscripts (MSS). The textual difficulty is considerable. The verb προσλαβοῦ 'receive' appears in three different positions in the MSS and in some MSS not at all. Also, some MSS read σοί 'to you'; others instead read σὺ δέ 'And you'; still others include all three words, σοι σὺ δέ '. . . to you. And you. . . .' The oldest MS we have with σὺ δέ and without σοί is from the ninth century, the oldest with σοί and without σὺ δέ is from the fourth century, and the oldest with both is from the sixth century. So, if we were to base our judgment on MS age, we might follow the text chosen by UBS, containing σοί, but not σὺ δέ.

It might be argued that the original text included προσλαβοῦ 'receive', as the Textus Receptus and many MSS do. If this were so, it would be hard to understand how it was ever omitted, or how it came to be in different positions in different MSS. Also regarding προσλαβοῦ, for those texts that contain σὺ δέ or σοι σὺ δέ but do not contain προσλαβοῦ, the resultant construction requires that an implied προσλαβοῦ be understood as the verb of the construction. But Paul is more likely to have delayed any reference to the request to receive (προσλαβοῦ) Onesimus as himself until he had first stressed the closeness of his relationship with him. Such was Paul's tact that he is unlikely even to have begun the statement of his request until he had given sufficient grounds for Philemon to think well of Onesimus. This argument, of course, applies with even more force against the explicit inclusion of προσλαβοῦ 'receive' at this point in the text. The UBS text does not include προσλαβοῦ explicitly nor require its implicit inclusion. Moreover, the hortatory paragraph pattern based on the UBS text and as presented in this SSA is certainly a well-structured one.

I am sending him back Ἀναπέμπω may mean either 'send up, refer (someone to one in authority)' in a legal sense, or 'send back'. There is no doubt that it at least refers to the physical sending of Onesimus back to Philemon, since Philemon is told to receive him in 17. If there is also the thought of referring Onesimus' case here, the referring is to no one other than Philemon, as σοί 'to you(sg)' (immediately following ἀνέπεμψα) shows. This word stands as the main verb of the *basis* unit 12-16, and it is highly probable that the main verb of the APPEAL unit stands in a reciprocal relationship to it. That verb is προσλαβοῦ 'receive', a definite reciprocal of 'send back' rather than the reciprocal of 'refer', which might be 'decide (his case in love)', for instance.

The literal meaning of the form ἀνέπεμψα is 'I have sent back'. It is an epistolary aorist written from the time perspective of the recipient of the letter rather than from the time perspective of the writer. When Philemon reads the letter, Onesimus will already have been sent back to him. In English, however, we would use a present tense here, and so this is used in the display text. Note, though, that there may be other languages which would follow the Greek pattern or might even use a future tense.

this one who is The syntax of αὐτόν 'him' (which agrees with the relative ὅν 'whom') is unusual here. It has been explained as a Hebraism corresponding to the Hebrew relative clause construction, but this occurs nowhere else in Paul's writings. It also has been explained as resumptive, introducing τοῦτ' ἔστιν 'that is' after the intervening σοί 'to you' in order to clarify who it is that he is referring to in τὰ ἐμὰ σπλάγχνα 'my own heart'. While it is true that αὐτόν would have that function here, it seems hardly necessary for this purpose alone, because in the New Testament the phrase introduced by τοῦτ' ἔστιν universally takes the case of its antecedent. That is, to refer to σοί, Paul would have to write τοῖς ἐμοῖς σπλάγχνοις anyway. More likely it is intensive, as in 1 Pet. 2:24, and used for emphasis, to indicate Paul's emotional attitude toward Onesimus.

The Greek τοῦτ' ἔστιν 'that is' is a set form that introduces some kind of explanation of what went before. Here Paul goes on to explain that his emotional attitude toward Onesimus is one of great affection.

***as dear to me as* my own self [SYN/MTY]**
'My own heart', 'my very own heart', 'my very heart' are all possible translations of τὰ ἐμὰ σπλάγχνα, since the use of the possessive adjective ἐμά rather than the possessive pronoun μου emphasizes the possession, 'my own'.

By making the point here that Onesimus is 'my very own heart', Paul can say in 17b, 'receive him as me'. Note how 12 and 17b relate as reciprocal actions, 'I am sending Onesimus back to you, sending my very own heart; therefore, receive him as you would receive me'. 'Heart' is a figure of speech; it may be either synecdoche or metonymy here. One choice for the propositionalization would be to take it as synecdoche, the heart standing for the whole person, and translate it nonfiguratively as 'my very own self'. But in doing so, we would be using another figure of speech by referring to one person as another. A second choice would be to take 'my very own heart' as metonymy, the heart standing for the faculties associated with the heart (or, in Greek, vital organs) and translate, for instance, as 'this one who is extremely dear to me'. A third choice would be to use a combination of both of these: 'who is as dear to me as my own self'. This choice is used in the display text because it more clearly maintains the relationship between 'my very own heart' and 'receive him as me' that is found in the original.

13a I would have liked to keep him with me The form ἐβουλόμην 'I would have liked' here in v. 13 is referred to by Greenlee (1986:49) as an example of the type of imperfect which indicates an "impossible, impractical, or hesitant wish." An alternate view that it means 'for a time I was inclined to, but then I decided otherwise' (cf. 2 Cor. 1:15) pictures Paul as entertaining the possibility for a while before deciding against it. Lightfoot (1879) says in favor of the first interpretation, "The imperfect of this and similar verbs are not infrequently used where the wish is stopped at the outset by some antecedent consideration which renders it impossible, and thus practically it is not entertained at all. . . . So here a not improbable meaning would be not 'I was desirous', but 'I could have desired'." The fact that Paul seems to state in v. 14 a principle that forms his basis of action in such cases as this supports Greenlee's and Lightfoot's interpretation. This is followed in the display text, 'I would have liked'.

13c while *I am* a prisoner *because I preach* the gospel Here again as in v. 10, the Greek text has ἐν τοῖς δεσμοῖς, literally, 'in the chains'.

14a *because* you had not *yet been asked by me and* consented *that I keep him here with me* The phrase χωρὶς . . . τῆς σῆς γνώμης 'without your consent' may seem simple enough to understand, but does Paul mean that (1) Philemon withheld his consent or (2) he had not yet given his consent because he had not known about the situation and had not yet been asked by Paul? It seems quite obvious from the context that the latter is the case. The difference between (1) and (2) is that there is a missing step in (1). This is brought out in the display text: '*because* you had not <u>*yet been asked by me and*</u> consented *that I keep him here with me*'. In some languages the missing step will not need to be filled in, but in others it may be ambiguous if that step is left out.

I decided not to keep him here at all Regarding οὐδὲν ἠθέλησα ποιῆσαι 'I decided to do nothing', the semantic structure of 13-14, both relationally and content-wise, is such that in the display text and, no doubt, in many languages it would be much clearer and more natural to translate this phrase specifically rather than generically, for example, 'I decided not to keep him here' or 'I decided not to keep him here at all'. The use of οὐδέν 'nothing' would certainly seem to indicate that Paul is not going to do one thing without Philemon's consent, whether it be retaining him for just a little while longer before sending him back or writing a letter to Philemon asking if he may retain him. Therefore, it would seem best to retain the force of 'nothing' in the display text and, where necessary, translate as 'I decided not to keep him here with me at all' or 'I decided not to keep him here even for a little while'.

14b-c *I decided that I should* **not force you to help** *me in this situation*; *I decided that you should help me only if you* **really wanted to help** *me* To what does τὸ ἀγαθόν σου 'your good (deed)' refer? It most likely does not refer to Philemon's consent to allow Onesimus to stay with Paul. It is true that the only specific actions in focus in 13 and 14 have to do with Paul's keeping Onesimus, and Philemon's agreement or disagreement with that. But that Paul does not see this as a possible future action is shown by the fact that by the time Philemon finds out anything about Onesimus' having been with Paul, Onesimus will already be back with Philemon. Paul has decided not to allow Philemon to act under compulsion and so is sending Onesimus back to Philemon. In so doing he does not give Philemon the chance to act under his own free will as far as Paul's retention of Onesimus is concerned; he has already sent him back. If he had temporarily kept Onesimus and sent a letter to Philemon saying he was willing to return him or keep him, whichever Philemon wished, then Philemon would have had more of a chance to act of his own free will. Nor does it really seem that Paul was thinking of Philemon sending Onesimus back. The whole thrust of the rest of the letter has to do with Paul's persuading Philemon to receive Onesimus back in a loving, Christian way.

So it would seem that Paul is stating a principle in this ἵνα clause (14b-c). He may be intending that it be understood as a general principle applying to all situations ('any good deed you do'). Or he may be applying that principle specifically to this case of keeping or not keeping Onesimus, a case in which the second part of the principle, willingly doing the good deed, is in actuality eclipsed by Paul's action in carrying out the first part of the principle, not forcing the good deed to be done. This latter interpretation, that is, the principle's application to this particular situation, is followed in the display text since 13-14 are focusing on this situation: '*I decided that I should* not force you to help *me in this situation*; *I decided that you should help me only if you* really wanted to help *me*'. Note that the first part of the principle is realized, while the second part is still only Paul's stating of the way he handles such situations as a general principle.

Because of this, the second part of the ἵνα construction, which in its full manifestation would be 'but (that your good deed be done) willingly', is not a true purpose of 'I decided to do nothing'. The first part is a true purpose, but since the first and second parts of this ἵνα construction are closely bound together, it was decided to treat them in a similar manner. The ἵνα construction functions as amplification in the propositionalized relational structure.

15a *God permitted that* **Onesimus leave** *you* The form ἐχωρίσθη may be taken as an aorist passive with the meaning 'he was separated (from you)'; or it may be taken as an aorist middle, 'he parted (from you)', which is essentially an active construction in most languages. The word has this active sense in most, if not all, of its other occurrences in the New Testament in this middle/passive form (Acts 1:4; 18:1, 2; Heb. 7:26; 1 Cor. 7:10, 11, 15a, 15b). However, in this context, it cannot be understood that Onesimus himself wished to part from Philemon for a while in order that he might be with him forever. This was not his purpose in leaving Philemon. So any translation that implies this would not be accurate.

If it is taken as a passive, as many commentaries and versions do, it is difficult in the context of the gospel to see any other purposer in mind than God himself. In the display text here, ἐχωρίσθη is taken as a passive and 'God' is supplied as the one who allows or causes the separation. There are at least two other possible renderings. One is to use the passive without supplying 'God'. The other is to use a form such as in NEB, "Perhaps this is why you lost him for a time, that you might have him back for good. . . ." But any translation is wrong which implies that Onesimus' own purpose in running away was so that he might be taken back forever or which implies that someone else other than God was purposing this. Another danger is that the translation might come across as nonsense because the purpose does not appear to be in a logical relationship with the means.

A final question would be whether God's action should be seen as causing the separation or permitting the separation. Since Paul tempers his statement here with 'perhaps', it probably is better to use 'permitted' rather than 'caused'.

for this *very* purpose The use of διὰ τοῦτο 'because of this, for this purpose' and its forefronting before the verb show that it is marking the ἵνα purpose clause (15b) as prominent, 'Perhaps he was separated from you for a little while for the very purpose that you might have him back again forever. . . .'

15b *he would believe in Christ, and as a result* Though 'God' is supplied as the purposer in v. 15, there is still a logical step missing in 'perhaps God permitted that he leave you for a little while in order that you might have him back forever'. That is the step of Onesimus' meeting Paul and coming to Christ (cf. v. 10). Without this logical step, the reasoning falls apart; yet in Greek and many languages it may be left implicit and the complete reasoning chain still be understood. For other languages, its omission will only result in nonsense. As an important part of the logical sequence, it is made explicit in the display text, or at least partially so.

you would have him back Lightfoot (1879) notes that ἀπέχειν in this context "may bear either of two senses: (1) 'to have back, to have in return': or (2) 'to have to the full, to have wholly'. . . . In other words the prominent idea in the word may be either *restitution*, or *completeness*." However, the context indicates that both ideas are present. The fact that Onesimus was Philemon's slave and departed from him means that ἀπέχῃς must at least refer to Philemon's *receiving him back* or *having him back*, while αἰώνιον 'forever' indicates the completeness of the possession, at least as far as time is concerned.

forever There is not much support in the commentaries or otherwise for translating αἰώνιον 'eternal, eternally' as only referring to this life, though a few commentators do support that position. The relationship of a beloved brother in the Lord (16) is one that continues eternally, and there is no reason why Paul would not be intending to refer to the full length of that relationship.

16 Verse 16 is in an amplificatory relation with v. 15. It goes on to describe Philemon's new relationship with Onesimus—Philemon will have him no longer as a slave but as a dear brother.

What should be the tense/mood for v. 16 in the propositionalization? There are no verbs in this verse; the verse appears to function as a continuation of the purpose construction that begins in 15b. But continued use of 'would' in 16 sounds too uncertain and unnatural in this context in English. Interestingly enough, we find that the Greek negative used in 16 is not μηκέτι 'no longer' which generally occurs in subjunctive constructions but οὐκέτι 'no longer' which generally occurs in indicative constructions. It seems to be going too far to say as Lightfoot, "The negative is not μηκέτι, but οὐκέτι. The negation is thus wholly independent of ἵνα . . . ἀπέχῃς." Still, there is an element of the indicative mood in 16. Thus 'will' is used in the propositionalization rather than 'would'.

16a *no longer as a slave only* The position of ὡς 'as' after αἰώνιον αὐτὸν ἀπέχῃς 'you might have him back forever' suggests the sense of ὡς described by BAGD, p. 898, entry III, as introducing "the characteristic quality of a person, thing, or action, etc., referred to in the context." When people are concerned, ὡς may introduce the role or position they fill. Phlm. 16 is, in fact, listed under entry III in BAGD. Some of the references listed under this sense refer to cases where the comparative sense of ὡς (its primary meaning?) is not present at all. But in other cases it is rather difficult to disambiguate the two senses, as in the following two references listed under the 'characteristic quality' sense: 1 Cor. 3:10 ὡς σοφὸς ἀρχιτέκτων θεμέλιον ἔθηκα 'as a wise master builder I laid a foundation', which could also be understood as 'similar to/like a wise master builder I laid a foundation'; and 1 Pet. 2:2 ὡς ἀρτιγέννητα βρέφη τὸ λογικὸν ἄδολον γάλα ἐπιποθήσατε 'as newborn children, crave pure spiritual milk', which NIV translates, "*like* newborn babies, crave pure spiritual milk [emphasis added]."

No doubt the same thing is happening here in Phlm. 16. Only the context and situation itself can reveal whether οὐκέτι ὡς δοῦλον means 'no longer in the (legal) position of a slave' or 'no longer like a slave'. If this is true, Vincent (1897) is almost right when he says, "Paul does not say that Philemon is to receive Onesimus freed, and no longer a slave, which would be δοῦλον simply, but that, whether he shall remain a slave or not, he will no longer be regarded *as* a slave, but as a brother beloved." It would be more correct to say that if Paul wanted Philemon to know for sure that he was directly requesting Philemon to free Onesimus (and certainly in such a critical matter he would have had to have been clear), he would not have used ὡς, because ὡς is too ambiguous.

Also, if Paul were asking Philemon to release Onesimus immediately, it is difficult to see how he could say in v. 11, 'Formerly he was useless to you, but now he is useful to you. . . .' The question of whether or not Paul hoped that the final outcome would be Onesimus' legal freedom somewhere down the road is a different question (see 21c). '*Only*' in the display text makes it clear that Paul is not suggesting outright that Onesimus be granted his freedom.

16c but *he certainly will be* more *dear* to you *than he is to me* 'Certainly' is used to propositionalize the component of intensity which is signaled in the Greek text by the use of πόσῳ 'how much'. The use of πόσῳ in Greek is similar to the use of 'how much' in English to indicate intensity. But since this is basically a question form being used for something other than a question, it is not used in that form in the display text.

16d *since he* not only belongs to the Lord but *he* also belongs to you In the construction 'how much more to you both in the flesh and in the Lord', it seems very likely that 'in the flesh' refers to those human relationships arising from the master-servant relationship that Philemon has with Onesimus, a relationship which Paul does not have with him. But Paul does have a very close relationship with Onesimus in the Lord, as verses such as 10 and 12 show. Therefore, we must ask what Paul means by 'how much more to you both in the flesh and in the Lord'. Does he mean (1) that Philemon's relationship with Onesimus will be a dearer one than Paul's, both in the spheres of the flesh and of the Lord, or does he mean (2) that Philemon's relationship with Onesimus will be a dearer one because it is not only a relationship in the Lord but it is also a relationship in the flesh? If the first interpretation is the right one, how would Philemon have a dearer relationship than Paul in the Lord? Was Paul thinking of the fact that Onesimus would be with Philemon constantly and therefore a deeper relationship would develop?

The καί . . . καί construction, which is normally translated as 'both . . . and' but also may be translated as 'not only . . . but also' in some contexts (BAGD, p. 393, entry I.6), can be used in situations where the two parties have one element or ability in common but not the other, as in the second interpretation. In Mt. 10:28, the disciples are told not to fear the ones who can destroy the body but not the soul but to fear the one who can destroy καὶ ψυχὴν καὶ σῶμα 'both soul and body'. This might also be translated as 'the one who can destroy not only the body but also the soul' (or 'the soul as well as the body'). Notice, however, the reversal in order in English translation that must take place in Mt. 10:28 when using the 'not only . . . but also' construction. This reversal is exactly what must happen in Phlm. 16, 'how much more to you, not only in the Lord but also in the flesh'. In both examples it is the constituent that is crucial in the situation (i.e., the additional element or ability that the other party does not have) that comes first in the Greek, which is the essence of forefronting for prominence. Is καί . . . καί a construction that a Greek writer can use when he is referring to a 'not only . . . but also' situation but wants to reverse the order of the constituents for prominence (or some other reason)?

It is the second interpretation that is used in the display since it seems to fit the context and situation better and it also seems to have a plausible grammatical basis. Interpretation 1 has a grammatical basis that would certainly be possible but its contextual basis is questionable. A possible propositionalization of interpretation 1 is: 'but *he certainly will be* more *dear* to you *than he is to me, since he* belongs to you and *also since you will be able to fellowship with him* as a Christian brother *more closely than I will be able to*'.

Grounds rather than reason The communication relation signaled by the ἐν prepositional phrases here has been analyzed as grounds rather than reason since the effect, '*he* certainly *will be* more *dear* to you *than he is to me*', is future and almost prescriptive rather than being completely referential.

SECTION CONSTITUENT 17 (Propositional Cluster: Appeal for 12–21)

THEME: *If you consider me your partner, receive Onesimus as you would receive me.*	
RELATIONAL STRUCTURE	CONTENTS
┌─ grounds ───────	17a Therefore, if you consider me *your* partner,
└─ EXHORTATION ───	17b receive him [Onesimus] as *you would receive* me.
See p. 48 for vv. 18–19.	

PROMINENCE AND THEME

Even though 17a was not chosen to appear in the higher-level theme statements, nevertheless it is an important part of the argument, so at this lower level it is included in the theme statement.

NOTES

17a Therefore, if The combination εἰ οὖν, literally 'if therefore' but semantically better ordered as 'therefore, if', signals that both the basis material coming before this clause (12–16) and the basis (grounds) material in the εἰ clause (17a) itself support the statement in the main clause (17b), i.e., the *APPEAL*. Often the content of the εἰ clause when it co-occurs with οὖν is a summary or restatement of the preceding support. In those cases, εἰ is rendered 'since' in the propositionalization because there is no conditionality involved. Here, however, Paul has not made direct reference in 12–16 to his partnership with Philemon or focused on that as one of his points of support for the *APPEAL*.

Although in the majority of cases where the combination εἰ οὖν occurs in the New Testament the εἰ clause does not signal condition at all (Mt. 7:11 and 22:45; Lk. 11:13 and 12:26; Jn. 13:14 and 18:8; Acts 11:17; Col. 3:1), there are three occurrences (Mt. 6:23; Lk. 11:36; 16:11) where condition is involved. Here in Philemon, Paul can assert the degree of his own love for Onesimus (in vv. 12 and 16, for instance) and his love for and partnership with Philemon (v. 1), but it seems best for him to use a construction that is potentially conditional to refer to Philemon's viewpoint regarding their partnership, since it is a matter of Philemon's own will, even though Paul knows that Philemon does consider him as his partner. In the display diagram, 17a is labeled as grounds and 'if' is used in the display text. (Although this condition might be seen as rhetorical, note that even true conditions may act as grounds if the condition is fulfilled.)

For translation into other languages, in general a word such as 'if' should not be used if it would indicate that Paul had grave doubts about Philemon considering him a partner. In those languages where a choice can be made, as in English, between 'since' and 'if', 'if' would probably be the better choice, other things being equal. In those languages where the semantic structure is somewhat different and it will not just be a case whether to use 'if' or 'since', keeping the form rhetorically conditional may be the best. In any case, 17a must be understood as a grounds, or *basis*, unit in the logical argument, that is, as support for the *APPEAL* in 17b.

you consider me Does με ἔχεις κοινωνόν mean 'you have me as a partner' or 'you hold/consider me a partner'? Ἔχω can mean either 'have' or 'hold', and the latter may be translated as 'count' (KJV, NEB) or 'consider' (RSV, NIV) when ἔχω occurs "w[ith] acc[usative] as obj[ect] and predicate a[ccusative]" (BAGD, p. 333, entry I.5), as here (cf. Mt. 14:5 and 21:26). Note, however, that in Acts 13:5 εἶχον (δὲ καὶ) Ἰωάννην ὑπηρέτην, the same type of construction, would be translated as 'they had John as an assistant' rather than 'they considered John as an assistant'. It is the context which determines whether the intended meaning is 'have' or 'hold/consider'. In 17, the onus is put squarely on Philemon. He is the one who must act. Notice that he is not only the subject of the verb denoting the action, προσλαβοῦ 'receive', but also the subject of ἔχεις 'have/hold'. Therefore, it seems somewhat more likely that the focus is on Philemon's standpoint in the relationship, that is, 'if you *consider* me as a partner', rather than Paul's standpoint, 'if/since you have me as a partner'.

partner Words from the κοινων- stem have the senses of 'sharing, participation, fellowship, close relationship'. Κοινωνός, the word used here, means 'partner', i.e., one who takes part in something with someone else. The use of κοινωνία in 1 Jn. 1:3, "We proclaim to you what we have seen and heard, so that you also may have fellowship with us" (NIV; cf. 1 Jn. 1:7), shows that all true believers have κοινωνία 'fellowship' with one another and are therefore κοινωνοί 'partners' in one sense.

The partnership being referred to here appears more specific than that which all Christians have in common. Onesimus himself is now a Christian and so would be that type of partner. But the basic focus of Paul's argument in this central part of the epistle (12-17) is on bringing Onesimus into the benefits of a partnership that he is otherwise on the outside of, even as a Christian. If Paul were merely thinking of Christian fellowship, he could have said, 'Since he is now your partner, receive him as you should receive a Christian partner'. But he asks for Onesimus the benefits of partnership *through* his own partnership with Philemon.

It would seem that this partnership is one based on the fact that Paul led Philemon to the Lord (19), and it also most likely refers to a partnership in the work of the Lord, as συνεργός 'fellow worker' in v. 1 suggests. We cannot be sure that Paul and Philemon worked together in the same location, though that is possible. But Paul at least thinks of Philemon as his fellow worker and partner in the work of the Lord in a specific way rather than merely purely generically as all Christians should be, and he believes Philemon thinks of him in the same way, as 17a shows.

17b receive This occurrence of προσλαβοῦ as used in Phlm. 17 is listed by BAGD, p. 717, entry 2.b, under the sense "*receive* or *accept in one's society, in(to) one's home* or *circle of acquaintances* τινά *someone*." The best commentary on its meaning here is, of course, ὡς ἐμέ 'as *you would receive* me' and 'as a dear brother' (v. 16).

as *you would receive* me The Greek text for 17b is προσλαβοῦ αὐτὸν ὡς ἐμέ 'receive him as me'. The phrase ὡς ἐμέ 'as me' is elliptical and could be propositionalized as either 'as *you would receive* me' or 'as *if he were* me'.

SECTION CONSTITUENT 18–19 (Paragraph: Basis₂ for the appeal of 17)

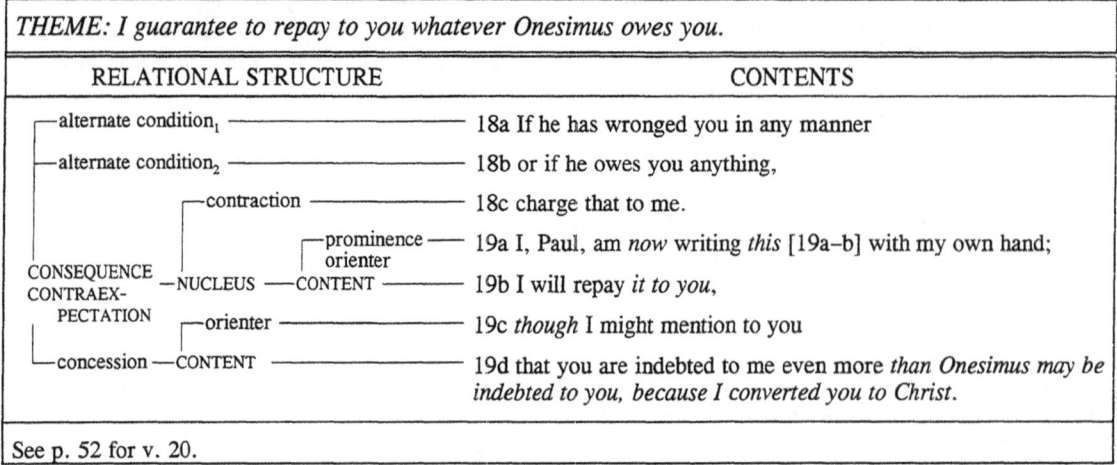

See p. 52 for v. 20.

PROMINENCE AND THEME

NUCLEUS 19b is the most naturally prominent constituent of the unit, but without some statement of the condition (18a–b), 19b really has no reference. The concession (19c–d), however, is not added to the theme statement, though it is also strongly motivational.

NOTES

18 The function of δέ at the beginning of 18 It would appear that δέ anticipates the potential opposition in the mind of Philemon to the APPEAL in 17. Thus it marks the beginning of the *refutation*. As mentioned earlier, the refutation was an important part of Greco-Roman rhetoric, dealing with known or anticipated objections the audience might have to the writer's appeal or thesis.

If he has wronged you in any manner, or ... owes you anything The εἰ ... τι 'if ... anything' construction here is one that is both hypothetical and comprehensive. The use of an alternation construction here, 'wronged you in any manner *or* owes you anything' increases the comprehensiveness of the statement. Although Paul may know or suspect one single action, he presents the case in a hypothetical way that includes the possibility of all kinds of actions, though not necessarily suggesting that Onesimus did more than one (or even any). Therefore, the semantic structure of the construction involving the two verbs ἠδίκησεν 'he wronged' and ὀφείλει 'he owes' is not propositionalized as if these actions/events were equivalent or as if the second were the specific of the first. The relation is alternation, 'If he has wronged you in any manner or if he owes you anything'. At the same time, when it comes to translation, the word used to translate ἠδίκησεν 'he wronged' must be the type of action that is repayable, since Paul says that he will repay whatever it may be.

Here again, as with the εἰ 'if' in 17a, there is the problem of whether Paul intended conditionality or not. As mentioned before, the Greek construction used here indicates universality, translatable into English as (1) 'if he has wronged you in any way or owes you anything' or (2) 'whatever wrong he might have done to you or whatever he owes you'. It is impossible from the Greek text or the context to know whether Paul actually knew that Onesimus had taken something from Philemon or not. But if Onesimus had made a true confession when he repented and accepted Christ, he likely would have revealed to Paul any offense he had committed against Philemon. Either of these two renderings is therefore acceptable. The construction with 'if' is more generic both in Greek and English because it may be used whether or not Paul knew Onesimus wronged Philemon or took anything from Philemon, while 'whatever wrong he might have done' is slightly less conditional and 'since' rather than 'if' would not be conditional at all. There are possible reasons why Paul might want to present this statement in conditional form; for example, as Lenski (1937) says, "The conditional form leaves it to Philemon to decide whether he, too, will consider that Onesimus did him a wrong and thus owes him the making good of that wrong." Note that the meaning of εἰ 'if' is not based upon Paul's actual knowledge or lack of knowledge of Onesimus' offense but upon the way that Paul chooses to present his argument to Philemon. However, in translation one would seek to avoid using an expression implying that Paul definitely did not know whether Onesimus has wronged Philemon or not. On the other hand, there would seem to be no reason why 'since' should be used rather than 'if' in this context.

wronged you . . . owes you anything There is much discussion in the commentaries on what Paul may have in mind when he talks about something that may be owed by Onesimus that he is willing to repay. Here are some of the possibilities given:

1. Onesimus may have stolen something outright (money or something else) from his master Philemon and then fled. Or he may have embezzled funds in some way.
2. Onesimus may have been sent on a journey by Philemon with money to purchase certain items. Perhaps Onesimus used the money for his own personal wants instead.
3. Onesimus may have owed money to Philemon even before he ran away.
4. Paul may be referring to the time lost from work during Onesimus' absence. "According to Rabbinical teaching a runaway slave who is recaptured must make good the time of his absence" (Oesterley 1910).

18c charge that to me An alternate rendering for 18c would be, 'consider/reckon that it is I who owe you that'.

Some commentators feel that Paul is not completely serious when he says, 'Charge that to me. I, Paul, write this with my own hand; I will repay it'. Alford (1865) says, ". . . hardly perhaps, notwithstanding the engagement of the next verse, with a view to actual repayment, but rather to inducing Philemon to forego exacting it." Meyer says of v. 18, "Friendly pleasantry which in ver. 19 becomes even jocular. . . ." Nonetheless it is the statement 'I, Paul, write this with my own hand' that is specifically used by Paul to assert the seriousness of what he is saying. That is the purpose of this type of orienter. Even though Paul may not have expected Philemon to ask for repayment, it would seem more likely than jocularity or friendly pleasantry that he was willing to do his best to repay, if Philemon should actually demand it of Onesimus. Friendly pleasantry and jocularity of this type are not appropriate to the argument of the epistle in general.

The relationship of 18c to 19a–b Is 18c in a contraction-amplification relationship with 19a–b or a CONCLUSION-grounds relationship? It is quite easy to see that 'charge that to me since I will repay it' makes a lot of sense. But there are good reasons for analyzing the relationship as other than CONCLUSION-grounds.

First, there is no conjunction marking a grounds relationship. Second, and more importantly, 'I will repay it' is a *commissive*. Paul is committing himself to a future action. 'Charge that to me' is a *directive*. Since commissives and directives both have affective roles (see Kathleen Callow 1998:110–15), it would appear that one does not necessarily have more prominence than the other and that one does not necessarily support the other when they occur contiguously. In fact, 'charge that to me' and 'I will repay it' are basically equivalent. Paul uses a directive and a commissive to say basically the same thing. Obviously, when he says, 'Charge that to me', he means nothing else than that he will repay it.

Since in this occurrence the commissive 'I will repay' is made prominent by 'I, Paul, am writing *this* with my own hand', it is more prominent than 'charge that to me', unless one follows the minority opinion that 'I, Paul, have written *this* with my own hand' refers back to 'charge that to me' rather than forward to 'I will repay'. The common use of 'I will repay' in Greek promissory notes (Graham 1983) also strongly suggests that this is the focal point of 18c–19b.

All these factors point to a contraction-amplification relationship in 18c–19b, one in which the amplification role is more prominent and thus labeled NUCLEUS.

19a I, Paul, am *now* writing *this* [19a–b] with my own hand When Paul says, 'I, Paul, have written with my own hand' (there is no 'this' in the Greek text), to how much of the text does he refer as being written by himself? The reason Paul mentions writing with his own hand here is that he is in effect signing a promissory note at this point, something that must be done with one's own hand. Not that the whole letter is a promissory note, but this small part acts as a promissory note. The aorist tense of ἔγραψα 'I have written' is either epistolary (like ἀνέπεμψα 'I have sent back' in v. 12) or documentary.

Lightfoot (1879) says, "The aorist is the tense commonly used in signatures; e.g. ὑπέργραψα to the conciliar decrees." Therefore, the reference need not be to something written previously, whether τοῦτο ἐμοὶ ἐλλόγα 'charge that to me' or the whole previous part of the epistle.

Graham (1983) says, "There are many examples of promissory notes from the times in which Paul lived. They usually use the words 'I will repay' in them and they are written in the person's own handwriting unless he was unable to write."

One might get the idea from some of the versions that all Paul wrote in his own hand was, 'I, Paul, will repay'. But the ordering of the Greek indicates that he also wrote the words 'I write with my own hand'. There is no way to know if Paul wrote more of the epistle with his own hand, but what is significant here is that he did write the 'promissory note' with his own hand to show that he really meant what he was saying.

now 'Now' is supplied in the display text to help signal that Paul has at this point picked up the pen to write with his own hand.

The role of 19a The purpose of 19a is to verify the truth of 19b, so 19a is a *prominence* orienter. Notice that according to the analysis in the preceding note, 19a is not an orienter in the ordinary sense of introducing the content of the writing, since the content of the writing is not only 19b but also 19a.

19c *though* I might mention to you

The construction in this clause begins with ἵνα, which normally introduces a purpose or content construction. Since ἵνα is followed by μὴ λέγω σοι, an indirect speech orienter, the whole expression would be translated literally as 'that/in order that I may not say to you'. But does this ἵνα construction really function as a purpose or content construction here? The best way to answer this is to determine its meaning. Literally it says, 'that I may not say/mention to you', but in fact it acts as an orienter to introduce the very words it says it will not say. Blass and Debrunner (1961, para. 495) mention this construction here in 19c-d as a possible instance of a "figure of thought" known as *paralipsis* in which "the orator pretends to pass over something which he in fact mentions." This would also come under the classification of an idiom since the meaning of this construction is different from the meaning conveyed by the individual words. RSV translates ἵνα μὴ λέγω σοι here with a somewhat similar idiom in English, 'to say nothing of'. It translates ἵνα μὴ λέγω ὑμεῖς (literally, 'that/in order that I not say about you(pl)') in 2 Cor. 9:4 similarly, 'to say nothing of you'. The fact that this same expression occurs more than once in Paul's writings with a similar sense suggests that it may be an established idiom.

As for the role of this ἵνα construction, we would not especially expect an utterance that is illogical in its literal form to fit the logical communication relation(s) that the literal forms normally represent. Therefore, we would not necessarily expect 19c-d to be a purpose construction. In the similar construction in 2 Cor. 9:4, ἵνα μὴ λέγω ὑμεῖς is certainly not a purpose construction. It is very difficult to see how Phlm. 19c-d could be the purpose or content of anything in the context whether explicit or implicit. The semantic relationship must be determined by the meaning in this context. The relationship between 18c-19b and 19c-d is one of contraexpectation-concession since Paul would not be expected to pay a debt to a person who owes him a greater debt, but Paul promises to pay it anyway. Notice Vincent's (1897) paraphrase, "This is my promise to repay it, signed with my own hand; though I might intimate that it is you who are my debtor for your very self . . ."—in other words, contraexpectation-concession.

Note, too, that Vincent handles the figure nonfiguratively in his paraphrase. In his notes he calls it "a sort of elliptical construction in which the writer delicately protests against saying something which he nevertheless does say" (i.e., paralipsis). What the μὴ λέγω 'I not say' signals in the figure, the carefully chosen word 'intimate' signals in the nonfigurative realization.

This construction appears to be an example of *understatement,* a technique defined by *The Reader's Digest Great Encyclopedic Dictionary* (1966) as "a statement deliberately worded so as to be unemphatic or restrained in tone, often used as a contrast to point up the significance of its contents." As will be seen in the notes on 19d, that construction has prominence markers of its own, so it is not surprising that its orienter (19c) would be constructed to reinforce that prominence.

Though understatement would typically be adjusted in an SSA, it is difficult to adjust this example to a direct emphatic statement since such wording would not have served the purposes of the author. Concluding that the prominence signals of the content (19d) would mark the necessary prominence sufficiently, our solution was to propositionalize v. 19c by using the neutral expression '(though) I might mention to you'. Of course, for any language that can use understatement appropriately in this context, that would be the best solution.

19d that you are indebted to me even more *than Onesimus may be indebted to you, because I converted you to Christ* Is 'you owe me your own self' figurative? A man could say that to his slave and it could possibly be understood nonfiguratively. But 19d should be treated as figurative since it refers to the spiritual sense of indebtedness; the debt is not that Philemon is really a possession of Paul but that he owes a giant debt of gratitude since, apparently, without Paul's efforts Philemon would not have been rescued from eternal death. Thus in the propositional display in Beekman and Callow (1974:366), this constituent is translated as 'you are indebted to me because I converted you'. The inherent meaning of σεαυτόν 'yourself' and the ascensive sense of καί 'even' ('even yourself') indicate that Philemon's debt to Paul is much greater than Onesimus' debt to Philemon. This emphasis needs to be retained in the propositionalization. Therefore, the rendering in the display text is, 'You are indebted to me even more *than Onesimus may be indebted to you, because I converted you to Christ*'. An alternate rendering might be, 'You are indebted to me even more *than Onesimus may be indebted to you, because you would be spiritually lost if I had not led/caused you to believe in Christ*'. 'Indebted' may not necessarily be a figure in English when applied to spiritual matters, but it may be in other languages, and so some adjustment may have to be made in translation. For example, a simile may be used, 'it is as if you are indebted to me'.

you are indebted to me The Greek word προσοφείλω is glossed by BAGD, p. 717, as "*owe besides*, though it is oft[en] scarcely poss[ible] to find any special force in the prep[osition] and to differentiate the compound fr[om] the simple verb [ὀφείλω]. . . ." It does not seem necessary to translate 'besides' in this verse. There has been no other debt mentioned of Philemon's to which this one would be additional.

Greenlee (1989) states that a number of commentators are of the general opinion that the προσ- of προσοφείλεις in this context does not indicate "an additional obligation, but rather an offsetting and greater obligation." If this is true, then προσοφείλεις is another indicator of the greater debt owed by Philemon and one can see why Paul would have chosen to use this form of the verb rather than the simple verb. In the display text this sense would be included in 'even more'.

SECTION CONSTITUENT 20 (Propositional Cluster: Basis₃ for the appeal of 17)

THEME: *Please encourage me in this matter as you encourage other believers in Christ.*		
RELATIONAL STRUCTURE		**CONTENTS**
┌─ generic ───────		20a Yes,* brother,* I want you to benefit me spiritually;
└─ SPECIFIC ───────		20b *specifically*, encourage me *by means of your receiving Onesimus properly, as you encourage other believers* in Christ.
See p. 55 for v. 21.		

PROMINENCE AND THEME

The nuclear 20b, which is a specific of 20a, should be the basic part of the theme. It would be appropriate, however, to retain the emphasis on 20b that is signaled by 20a. 'Please' is used to do this: 'Please encourage me in this matter as you encourage other believers in Christ'. 'In this matter' is used to keep the encouragement in the proper context, namely, the receiving of Onesimus properly.

NOTES

20a Yes,* brother* In BAGD, pp. 532–33, ναί 'yes' here is classified as a "particle denoting affirmation, agreement, or emphasis. . . . 3. in emphatic repetition of one's own statement *yes (indeed)*." It has reference to something that has been said before, and since v. 20 is asking that the basic APPEAL (17b) be carried out, it is likely that the direct reference is to the basic APPEAL and probably indirectly to the support for that APPEAL. 'Yes' emphasizes at this point the fact that Paul wants the basic APPEAL to be carried out.

The use of the emphatic ναί 'yes' in combination with the vocative ἀδελφέ 'brother' suggests a structural change. The two words introduce the emotional appeal. One would certainly expect a word indicating emphasis to introduce such an appeal. The denotation, and possibly connotation, of 'brother' also relates to the emotions, and the fact that Paul uses this vocative to introduce new units is well established. (Cf. 2 Thess. where ἀδελφοί 'brothers' is one of the introductory features in each of the four main sections of the body of the epistle; see John Callow 1982:26).

to benefit The verb in 20a is ὀναίμην, an optative form of ὀνίνημι. In BAGD, p. 570, the general meaning of this form, both for the New Testament and other early Christian literature, is glossed as "*may I have joy* or *profit* or *benefit, may I enjoy* w[ith] gen[itive] of the pers[on] or thing that is the source of the joy"; but for this specific reference in Philemon it is glossed as "*let me have some benefit from you in the Lord.*" Therefore, the word would appear to have two senses: 'to have benefit/profit' or 'to have joy'. Commentators (or at least most of them) do not mention the meaning of 'joy' for this reference (the only occurrence of the verb in the New Testament), but it should be noted that in the several times it occurs in Ignatius' writings it always, or at least very often, has the sense of 'joy'. Also, the verb in the parallel construction (20b), ἀνάπαυσον 'refresh, encourage', has a sense akin to 'have joy' or 'enjoy'. Since these two clauses appear almost equivalent in meaning otherwise, one might think that the sense 'have joy' would be the appropriate one.

But there are good reasons for understanding ὀναίμην in its sense of 'have benefit from, have profit from'. Many commentators see it as a play on words with Ὀνήσιμος. Oesterley (1910) says it "is a play on the name Onesimus." Ὀνήσιμος means 'useful' or 'profitable'. Furthermore, in a section that is built around the paying of debts, one might expect that the word ὀναίμην is used in the sense of 'profit' or 'benefit'. A comparison of 19d with 20a shows that there may well be a reciprocal relationship between these two verses:

19d καὶ σεαυτόν μοι προσοφείλεις
    even yourself to-me you-owe
      Philemon   Paul action

20a ἐγώ σου ὀναίμην ἐν κυρίῳ
    I of-you I-wish-profit in the-Lord
    Paul Philemon reciprocal action

'You owe your very self to me; I would like some profit/benefit from you'. The basis on which Paul can ask Philemon to benefit him in 20a is the fact that he has benefited Philemon, as seen in 19d.

Rather than being part of the same unit, however, it would appear that 19d is actually functioning as the tail in a tail-head link with 20, 20a being the head in that link.

Either 'profit' or 'benefit' could be used in the display text. 'Profit' would probably carry on the debit-credit theme of the larger unit better, but 'benefit' would be appropriate to the type of action Paul is asking—the proper reception of Onesimus. Therefore, 'benefit' has been used in the display text.

I want you to benefit me There may be a problem in translating this verse into certain languages. Because it is the emotional appeal, the emotional-type verb used to translate ἀνάπαυσον 'refresh, encourage' (and possibly also ὀναίμην 'may I have benefit') should be kept focal, that is, as the hortatory verb; while as far as the total situation is concerned, it is the event of receiving Onesimus in the correct way that is the focal hortatory action. Paul's encouragement would be a result of that action and thus secondary. It would be improper in a semantic structure analysis to change the emotional appeal structure of the verse. But it would seem proper to supply the implied means of the encouragement. Thus 'by means of your receiving Onesimus properly' occurs in italics in the display text of 20b. (It is put in 20b since it is more appropriate to the more specific constituent of v. 20.) It may be that in some languages the means construction will have to be in hortatory form and the benefit/encouragement in a purpose construction.

spiritually There appear to be at least two ways in which ἐν κυρίῳ 'in the Lord' may be understood. One would be to take ἐν κυρίῳ as motivational grounds for Paul's request in 20a, 'Yes, brother, I want you to benefit me since we both are united to the Lord' or 'since we both believe in the Lord'. This is certainly a common way to understand ἐν κυρίῳ 'in the Lord'. Many commentators would agree with this sense here, and it may be the correct one. However, there is a possibility that ἐν here may come under BAGD's classification I.5.d., p. 259, "to indicate the scope within which someth[ing] takes place or has taken place." Paul's argument in 18–19 revolves around the owing and paying of debts, both material and spiritual:

	Philemon	*Paul*
18–19b material debt (owed, promised to be paid)	he has wronged you/owes you	charge to me/I will repay
19d spiritual debt (owed to Paul)		you owe me yourself
20a spiritual debt (Paul asks for payment)	I want you to profit me in the Lord	

It may be, then, that when Paul uses ἐν κυρίῳ 'in the Lord' he is qualifying the profit as profit in the Lord, that is, spiritual profit rather than the material profit or exchange referred to in 18–19: 'I have benefited you in the Lord by bringing you to Christ; now benefit me in the Lord (or benefit me spiritually) by receiving Onesimus properly'. Note that in v. 16 there is a somewhat similar differentiation—ἐν σαρκὶ καὶ ἐν κυρίῳ 'in the flesh and in the Lord'.

One needs to ask, however, if ἐν Χριστῷ 'in Christ' in 20b has a similar sense; and if it does not, would that have bearing on the meaning of ἐν κυρίῳ 'in the Lord' in 20a, especially since the two halves of the verse seem at least in some sense to be equivalent? 'Encourage my heart in Christ' does not have any direct reference to the debt/pay/profit theme, so the reasons for analyzing ἐν as referring to the scope or sphere of that activity are not in focus. In 20b, we would expect that the encouragement would be in the sphere of the Christian life. It is an emotional thing, and our emotions are always dealt with in the Christian sphere. Paul would not be adding anything by putting 'in Christ' on the end of his statement, probably not even emphasis by this type of redundancy. What we might rather expect, then, is that Paul is using 'in Christ' for motivational reasons. Thus it does not seem necessary to take both ἐν 'in' phrases as having the exact same function or sense. Though both of the verbs of this verse content-wise refer to the result on Paul of Philemon's receiving Onesimus in the proper manner, they look at that result in a slightly different way—the first as a benefit which may be related to Philemon's spiritual debt, the second as encouragement and relief from anxiety.

In v. 7, Paul commends Philemon for encouraging the hearts of the saints—τὰ σπλάγχνα τῶν ἁγίων ἀναπέπαυται διὰ σοῦ 'the hearts of the saints have been encouraged by you'. The wording is quite similar to that here in 20b and there is no doubt that Paul means for Philemon to see the connection. In 20b, μου 'my' occurs before τὰ σπλάγχνα 'heart'. When the pronoun occurs before the noun in genitive constructions, it tends to indicate that the pronoun is being contrasted with some other pronoun or personal noun, or is being emphasized, or both. We would not usually expect such a contrast in the formal structure when the noun phrases are so far apart, but Paul no doubt is signaling that he, too, wants to be included among those whom Philemon encourages: 'You have encouraged the hearts of other Christians, how about encouraging *my* heart in Christ too'. Based on these considerations, we have propositionalized 'in Christ' in the following way: 'Encourage me . . . *as you encourage other believers* in Christ'.

An alternate way of handling this would be to make the agent of the encouragement in the second clause of 20b more generic: 'Encourage me *by means of your receiving Onesimus properly as/since fellow believers* in Christ *should encourage one another*'. However, if both ἐν phrases are taken in the same way, the propositionalization of 20 might be: 'Yes,* brother,* I want you to benefit me *since we both believe* in the Lord *Jesus; specifically,* encourage me *by means of your receiving Onesimus properly since we both believe* in Christ'. Note that when both ἐν phrases are taken in the same way, there is not much doubt that they both refer to Christ.

20b The relationship between 20a and 20b The two verbs ὀναίμην 'may I have profit' and ἀνάπαυσον 'refresh/encourage' are requesting Philemon to perform the same action, namely, to receive Onesimus properly, but content-wise they describe how performing that action will affect Paul. Thus it is possible that performing the one action could affect Paul in two different ways.

But it is more likely that the benefit Paul is talking about here refers to the encouragement of his heart. Therefore, 20b is no doubt a restatement of some kind of 20a, so there is either a NUCLEUS-equivalent or generic-specific relationship here. The benefit is not described in 20a, but in 20b. So the relationship is generic-specific, and the specificity of 20b suggests that it is more prominent than 20a. The fact that the verb in 20b is imperative and therefore probably has more natural prominence than the optative in 20a supports this decision.

encourage me The primary meaning of ἀναπαύω is 'to rest' and in the transitive construction, 'cause to rest'. In its combination with 'heart', it is often glossed as 'refresh'. 'Refresh my heart' is not used in the display text since 'heart' is a "dead" figure and the collocation 'refresh my heart' is not quite an appropriate one in modern-day English anyway. It is translated by BAGD, p. 59, entry 1, for this verse as "refresh, cheer my heart," and *The Twentieth Century New Testament* also renders it as "cheer my heart." TEV renders it as "cheer me up," while Beekman and Callow (1974) use "refresh" or "encourage." These are good generic translations; the display text in this SSA reads similarly, 'encourage me'. However, it should be pointed out that a translation such as "relieve my anxiety" (NEB) is more to the point and more specific to the context. And it may be that 'relieve' is closer to 'cause to rest' than 'encourage' or 'cheer' are. 'Relieve my anxiety' might have been used in the display text except that 'anxiety' is an abstract noun. But we might render it as 'cause me to no longer be anxious *about Onesimus*', though this would be more difficult to tie in with v. 7, which probably needs to be kept generic.

in Christ 'In Christ' has been discussed under the note 'spiritually' in 20a.

SECTION CONSTITUENT 21 (Propositional Cluster: Basis₄ for the appeal of 17)

THEME: I have written this letter to you confident of your compliance with my request.

RELATIONAL STRUCTURE	CONTENTS
RESULT	21a I have written *this letter* to you confidently,
REASON — NUCLEUS	21b *because* I know that you will comply with *what I am requesting that you do*;
— amplification	21c *in fact,* I know that you will do even more than what I am requesting *that you do.*

See p. 57 for v. 22

PROMINENCE AND THEME

The only finite verb in the Greek text of this verse is ἔγραψα 'I have written'. Normally this would indicate that 'I have written to you' is (or is the basic part of) the most prominent proposition in the verse. Also, the fact that the two participles depending upon ἔγραψα would appear to express reason, which is usually the less prominent role in a reason-result relationship, supports the assumption that 'I have written to you' is the most prominent proposition. However, when it comes to expressing the theme of the verse, it might also appear that 'I have written to you' could be left out and the remaining portion would still be the major point that Paul wanted to make: 'I am confident that you will comply with my request'. In addition, the fact that the participial phrase 'confident of your compliance' is forefronted in the Greek text marks it as prominent.

It may be that Paul uses 'I have written to you' as a signal of his closure of the argument (i.e., the hortatory section) of the epistle. This may possibly have something to do with its occurrence in finite form. In other words, v. 21 may have two functions: motivation through expressing confidence in Philemon's compliance with the APPEAL of 17 and the closure of the argument for that appeal. If one focuses attention only on the motivation function, the Greek signals of prominence may seem somewhat skewed. But if one understands that 21 has two functions, one might expect that the signals for natural prominence would be used for one of those functions and marked prominence for the other. The theme, then, is, 'I have written this letter to you confident of your compliance with my request'. 'This letter' is supplied to avoid the misconception that another earlier letter is being referred to by the use of the past tense.

NOTES

21a–b I have written As suggested in the 'Prominence and Theme' notes for this unit, ἔγραψα is rendered in the display text as 'I have written' rather than as an epistolary aorist, 'I am writing', since ἔγραψα is understood as signaling the closing of the support for the APPEAL of 17.

The relationship between 'I have written' and 'being confident of your obedience' At least two interpretations are possible:

1. The first interpretation is that 'Being confident of your obedience' has a manner relationship with 'I have written'. When the clause 'I have written to you confidently' is considered in isolation, it is obvious that 'confidently' has a manner function. But 'confidently' by itself is basically only an orienter. In a given context an author may feel that the addressee knows what the content (sphere) of the confidence is and so explain no further: he uses only the word 'confidently' in this case. Or, he may feel that he needs to make the content explicit—'confident of your obedience', for example. It is evident that if the orienter alone expresses manner, orienter plus content also does. The NIV, "confident of your obedience, I write to you," and NEB, "I write to you confident that you will meet my wishes," handle this manner relationship well. Propositionalization of manner constituents is sometimes difficult. One possibility here is to propositionalize by using the adverb 'confidently' in the result proposition and stating the content of the confidence in a reason proposition: 'I have written *this letter* to you confidently, *because* I know that you will comply with *what I am requesting that you do*'. Note that 'confident' must be repeated in some form (here, 'know') in the reason proposition.

2. The second interpretation is that 'Being confident of your obedience' is the reason for Paul writing to Philemon—'I have written to you *because* I am confident that you will obey/comply with *what I am requesting that you do*'.

It is the first interpretation that is followed in the display text because Paul's basic reason for writing to Philemon is not that he is confident that Philemon will obey but to persuade him to accept Onesimus in the proper way. In some languages there may be no way to say 'confident' or 'confidently' by itself, however, without adding the content of the confidence. But there will, no doubt, be other ways to handle a manner constituent, for example, a construction similar to the NEB rendering, with no conjunction at the beginning of the 'confident' clause and with or without the agent repeated in the 'confident' clause: 'I have written to you, I am confident that you will comply with what I have requested' or 'I have written to you, confident that you will comply with what I have requested'.

you will comply with *what I am requesting that you do* One of the exegetical problems in this verse is caused by what would seem to be an intuitive assumption that 'obedience' is the reciprocal of 'command', even though Paul has said that he prefers not to command Philemon in this situation (vv. 8-9). That ὑπακοή has a wider range of meaning than the English word 'obedience' is clear from the use of the verbal form, ὑπακούω, in the Septuagint translation of Is. 65:24: "Before they have called I will *respond*"; and also in Acts 12:13, "Peter knocked at the outer door and a servant girl named Rhoda came to *answer/respond*." If Philemon takes ὑπακοή in the context of the whole letter and especially of vv. 8-9, then he will understand it more in the sense of 'compliance' than 'obedience'.

Another possibility is that ὑπακοή refers to Philemon's obedient character in general. Vincent (1897) follows this interpretation in his paraphrase, "Being assured of your obedient spirit." There is a possibility that this is what Paul intended, but it would seem that there would be no way for Philemon to know whether Paul by 'your obedience' was referring to his obedient character in general or to his compliance with the requests of this letter. In fact, the primary meaning—the first meaning one thinks of—of 'confident of your obedience' in this context is compliance with Paul's request in this letter (at least in English, and I know of no reason why it should be different in Greek). Therefore, the propositionalization in the display text is, 'you will comply with *what I am requesting that you do*'. Another way to say this would be, 'I know that you will do *what I am requesting that you do*'.

21c *in fact,* **I know that you will do even more than what I am requesting** *that you do* What is Paul referring to when he says he knows that Philemon will do even more than he is asking him to do? Some commentators think that Paul is hoping Philemon will grant Onesimus legal freedom; others, that Paul is hoping Philemon will send Onesimus back to serve him. But perhaps Paul is just referring to special kindnesses that Philemon will show to Onesimus. There is really no way to know what Paul means. Thus in the display text it is left general.

DIVISION CONSTITUENT 22 (Paragraph: Closure of the body)

THEME: *Also, keep a guest room ready for me*	
¶ PTRN RELATIONAL STRUCTURE	CONTENTS
APPEAL	22a Also, keep a guest room ready for me,
┌─orienter	22b since I confidently expect
└─means	22c that by means of your(pl) praying *to God for me*,
basis ──RESULT	22d *he* will cause me to be released *and enable me to come* to you(pl).

See p. 59 for vv. 23–25.

PROMINENCE AND THEME

The *basis* unit is not included in the theme statement since it is an explanatory *basis* and therefore may have lower prominence than other types of *basis* units.

NOTES

See the comments on v. 22 in the section 'Structure and Boundaries' following the display of division constituent 12–21.

22a Also The word ἅμα, which is most often translated as 'at the same time' when it is acting as an adverb (as here), denotes an overlapping time relationship between the actions it relates. However, in some cases (e.g., Acts 24:26 *"At the same time* he hoped that money would be given him by Paul" [RSV, emphasis added]), the time relationship is more that of the durative type so that the relationship can also be seen as that of conjoined events rather than strictly simultaneous ones. Note that in Phlm. 22 the tenses of the two actions that ἅμα relates are different: προσλαβοῦ 'receive' in 17b is aorist, while ἑτοίμαζε 'prepare' here in 22a is present. It would seem that Paul is asking Philemon to be ready for his own coming over a period of time. 'At the same time' is not used in the display text in the attempt to avoid a suggestion of exact time correlation between the two actions involved. Since ἅμα δὲ καί may indicate conjoined relations and Paul is asking Philemon not only to receive Onesimus but also to prepare to receive Paul himself, 'also' is used to translate ἅμα δὲ καί. The NIV likewise translates the relationship as a conjoined one rather than strictly simultaneous, "And one thing more. . . ."

keep a guest room ready The imperative here, ἑτοίμαζε 'prepare', has a second person singular ending, whereas the other second person references in this verse are plural.

The verb ἑτοιμάζω is glossed by BAGD, p. 316, entry 1, as "*put* or *keep in readiness, prepare.*" As mentioned, the present tense here suggests preparation in some continuing sense. Note in contrast that all other occurrences of the imperative of this verb in the New Testament are in aorist form (see Mt. 3:3 and parallel passages Mk. 1:3 and Lk. 3:4; Mk. 14:15 and parallel passage Lk. 22:12; Lk. 17:8; Lk. 22:8; and Acts 23:23). An appropriate translation may be 'keep a guest room ready for me'.

guest room The most frequent meaning of ξενία in Greek literature was 'hospitality, entertainment', but it also had the sense of 'guest room'. In its only other use in the New Testament, in Acts 28:23, it most likely refers to a place (RSV has "lodging") rather than 'hospitality'. Most commentators and versions take it to refer to a guest room here in Philemon.

22b I confidently expect Elsewhere in SSAs 'confidently expect' has been used for ἐλπίζω or ἐλπίς "to avoid the implications of uncertainty that 'hope' often has in English usage" (John Callow 1983:105), and so we use it here also. Paul's request to Philemon to keep a guest room ready for him shows Paul's certainty that he will soon be released.

22d *he* will cause me to be released *and enable me to come* to you(pl) Two questions are associated with the Greek phrase χαρισθήσομαι ὑμῖν, literally, 'I will be granted to you'. The first has to do with the denotational meaning of this passage. Meaning number 1 given by BAGD, p. 876, for χαρίζομαι is "*give freely* or *graciously as a favor*"; this fits many contexts in the New Testament, especially where God or Christ is the agent. However, the use of this word in Acts 25:11, "no one has the right to *hand* me *over* to them," and Acts 25:16, "it is not the Roman custom to *hand over* any man before he has faced his accusers..." (NIV [emphasis added]), shows that in contexts where a prisoner or person being held by authorities is involved the word has the sense of 'hand over' or 'release'. And as these two references contrasted with Acts 3:14 show, this release may be either to those who want to kill the prisoner or to those who desire his freedom. In the context of Phlm. 22, Paul is a prisoner and he is referring to his release when he uses χαρισθήσομαι. At the same time, he states that this release will be through the prayers of the Colossians, so one cannot easily dismiss the sense of God graciously granting Paul his release (or graciously granting him to them).

The second question has to do with whether χαρισθήσομαι ὑμῖν means that Paul will be granted/released to them in the sense that he will be granted not only to be released but also to come all the way to Colossae, or if it means that he will be released in answer to their prayers, as in Acts 27:24 where κεχάρισταί σοι 'has granted to you' means 'God <u>has given</u> all those who sail with you safety <u>at your request</u>'.

Actually, both of these senses are realized in this context. Paul's release will be in answer to their prayers, and his request to Philemon to prepare for his coming shows that actual physical reception of Paul is also meant or implied.

Based on all these considerations, the following propositionalizations would be appropriate for this context:

1. I confidently expect that by means of your(pl) praying *to God for me, he* will cause me to be released *and enable me to come* to you(pl).
2. I confidently expect that by means of your(pl) praying *to God for me, he* will do what you(pl) ask him to do, *that is, he* will cause me to be released *and enable me to come to you(pl)*.

'Graciously' might be added before 'cause' in either 1 or 2.

Number 1 has been chosen for the display text since it is simpler than number 2; the release itself implies that their prayers will be answered so there is no need for the generic 'he will do what you ask him to do'. 'Enable me to come' is supplied in both options. In number 1 it is supplied because of the interpretation that 'to you' means actual physical reception; in number 2 it is supplied to fill in the step that is implied by Paul's request to Philemon to prepare for his coming in 22a. Of course, in any translation that follows the interpretation underlying propositionalization 2, 'enable me to come' may be omitted if it is deemed unnecessary.

EPISTLE CONSTITUENT 23–25 (Paragraph: Closing of the epistle)

THEME: Epaphras and my other fellow workers greet you(sg). May the Lord Jesus Christ bless you(pl) spiritually.

STRUCTURE			CONTENTS
GREETINGS		NUCLEUS₁	23 Epaphras, who *suffers hardship* with me in prison as one *who serves* Christ Jesus, greets you(sg).
		NUCLEUS₂	24 Mark, Aristarchus, Demas, and Luke, who are my *other* fellow workers, *also greet you(sg)*.
BENEDICTION			25 *I pray that* the Lord Jesus Christ *will continue to* bless you(pl) spiritually.

PROMINENCE AND THEME

There is no way to distinguish any levels in prominence between the GREETINGS and the BENEDICTION. Within the GREETINGS, Epaphras is mentioned separately from the others, the verb ἀσπάζεται 'he greets' is singular, and there is no occurrence of the verb in the plural to explicitly refer to the action of the other fellow workers greeting Philemon. (The others' performance of that action is only implicit.) These features seem to mark prominence on Epaphras, and so only he is mentioned by name in the theme statement.

NOTES

23 who *suffers hardship* with me in prison It is difficult to know exactly what Paul means when he calls Epaphras his συναιχμάλωτος 'fellow prisoner, fellow captive'. The options would appear to be:

1. Epaphras had been arrested and put in prison with Paul for some alleged offense arising from his preaching Christ or serving Christ in general and he was still there with Paul.
2. Epaphras had not actually been arrested himself, but was somehow sharing Paul's prison experience in order to minister to Paul's needs.
3. Epaphras had been in prison at some other time with Paul or had been in prison but not necessarily at the same time or place with Paul.
4. Paul is speaking completely figuratively as far as Epaphras' prison experience is concerned. Epaphras has either never been in prison or, if he has, Paul is not referring to that at all.

The strongest argument against number 1 is that in the greetings section in Col. 4 where Epaphras is mentioned, it is Aristarchus and not Epaphras whom Paul calls his συναιχμάλωτος 'fellow prisoner, fellow captive', while here it is the other way around. Since it is generally agreed that both epistles were written about the same time and certainly seem to have been sent at the same time, it is not likely that one of these men could have been freed and the other arrested in such a short period of time.

It seems more likely that Paul uses 'fellow prisoner' to mean either that Epaphras and he were closely associated in his present prison experience (number 2) or that 'fellow prisoner' is completely figurative (number 4). But the case for 'fellow prisoner' being purely a metaphor is not as clear-cut as for 'fellow soldier' in Phlm. 2. Paul certainly was not a literal soldier and Archippus probably was not either. But Paul really *was* a prisoner at the time of the writing of this epistle. Also, the idea of Christians being spiritual prisoners or captives is certainly not a common figure in Scripture.

Therefore, it seems better to understand 'fellow prisoner' as referring to Epaphras' sharing in the hardship of Paul's experience while ministering to him in whatever type of confinement he was experiencing (interpretation 2). This may have been a ministry that Epaphras and Aristarchus took turns at. And the closer Epaphras was involved in sharing Paul's hardships in prison the more significant is the meaning of 'fellow prisoner'.

An alternate interpretation (number 3) would be to understand that Epaphras had been in prison at some other time for the sake of the gospel, either with Paul or separately. This may possibly have been the case with Andronicus and Junias, for in Rom. 16:7 Paul calls them his συναιχμάλωτοι 'fellow prisoners', even though at the time he wrote the Epistle to the Romans Paul was not a prisoner. (There are no occurrences of this word in the New Testament other than in Col. 4:10, Rom. 16:7, and Phlm. 23.) But the problem with this interpretation for Phlm. 23 is that we do not know if Epaphras (or Aristarchus) was ever in prison, while we do know that Epaphras was involved with Paul in Paul's prison experience at the time of the writing of Philemon.

It is very difficult to know which of the four interpretations is best. The display text is based on interpretation 2, which is held by a number of commentators.

as one *who serves* Christ Jesus Earlier in the epistle Paul twice says that he is 'a prisoner of Christ Jesus' (δέσμιος Χριστοῦ Ἰησοῦ, vv. 1 and 9), and once he talks about being 'in the bonds of the gospel' (v. 13). In v. 23, now, he says Epaphras is his 'fellow prisoner in Christ Jesus' (ὁ συναιχμάλωτός μου ἐν Χριστῷ Ἰησοῦ), but since Paul is literally a prisoner, there is no way that this expression can be completely figurative.

The preposition ἐν 'in' often expresses the sphere within which something takes place or exists. There is little doubt that this is the meaning in view here. It is difficult to know the more specific sense Paul had in mind or even if he was thinking more specifically; therefore we must look to the context to understand how this should be propositionalized.

Graham (1983) notes that the translation "'who is my fellow-captive because he serves Christ Jesus'... makes it appear that Epaphras was also arrested because he was preaching about Christ" and that since this may or may not have been the case, "'who is serving Christ Jesus as my fellow-captive'" would be better. This is a good translation but its primary meaning may still be that Epaphras was actually a real prisoner or captive.

Since the SSA propositionalizations are based on the interpretation in the notes, the propositionalization we have chosen is 'who *suffers hardship* with me in prison as one *who serves* Christ Jesus'. 'As' is used here in its sense of marking role, not comparison.

It may be that in some languages more specific conjunctions or relations will have to be used. Note that 'who *suffers hardship* with me in prison because he serves Christ Jesus' does not directly suggest that his suffering hardship in prison with Paul was because he was arrested in his service for Christ.

24 Aristarchus, Demas Aristarchus is mentioned in Acts 19:29, 20:4, 27:2, and Col. 4:10. Demas is mentioned in Col. 4:14 and 2 Tim. 4:10.

Should Jesus who is called Justus also be included in the list of Paul's fellow workers? Since Paul's letters to the Colossians and to Philemon were written at the same time and sent together (Col. 4:7-9) to Colossae, and since those to whom Paul sends greetings are clearly the same in both epistles except for 'Jesus who is called Justus' (mentioned only in Colossians), a few commentators believe that the Greek text here should be punctuated ὁ συναιχμάλωτός μου ἐν Χριστῷ, (that is, with a comma after Χριστῷ), that the final -ς of Ἰησοῦς was omitted due to an oversight, and thus that 'Jesus' here actually refers to Jesus called Justus rather than to the full name 'Christ Jesus'. The fact that this interpretation has to propose a change in the text is one of its weaknesses. Also, it relies on the fact that the name of Jesus would need to be at the head of the list (after Epaphras); and since there is nothing in Colossians that would suggest a basis for his name being at the head of the list, there is no support for its position from that standpoint. Indeed, if Paul were a careful writer he would not have placed the name 'Jesus' right after 'Christ' (even though they would have been in different grammatical cases) lest ambiguity result.

Those who argue for a reference to Jesus who is called Justus point out that in the other two places where Χριστῷ occurs with ἐν 'in' in Philemon (8, 20) it is not followed by Ἰησοῦ. However, 'Christ Jesus' does occur elsewhere in the epistle (1, 9). Furthermore, the very fact that Christ is referred to in so many ways ('Lord Jesus Christ' 3, 25; 'Lord Jesus' 5; 'Christ' 6; 'Lord' 16, 20, besides those already mentioned) shows that we cannot place very much value on the argument that ἐν Χριστῷ Ἰησοῦ does not occur elsewhere in the epistle, only ἐν Χριστῷ.

25 you(pl) spiritually Note that τοῦ πνεύματος 'spirit' is singular though the pronoun is plural, 'your(pl) spirit'. It would appear that Paul regularly uses πνεῦμα 'spirit' in the *singular* to refer to the spirits or inner beings of a plurality of people, for example, in the other final benedictions similar to this one (Gal. 6:18 and Phil. 4:23) and also 1 Cor. 16:18 and Rom. 8:16. Rom. 8:16, especially, clearly indicates a situation where our individual spirits are being referred to, even though the Greek text uses a singular form with the plural pronoun: 'The Spirit himself bears witness with our spirit (τῷ πνεύματι ἡμῶν) that we are children of God'. This bearing witness is done on an individual basis with each person's spirit; thus when Paul refers to 'our spirit', he is not talking about spirit as a single entity but each of our individual spirits. Eph. 4:23 contains a similar phrase, mind (νοός) being a singular noun modified by the second person plural possessive pronoun ὑμῶν, with 'spirit' also being singular: 'be renewed in the spirit of your(pl) mind'. So, here too in Philemon, Paul is not talking about spirit as a single entity but the spirits of each of those to whom he is writing.

you(pl) It is most natural to take ὑμῶν 'your(pl)' here as referring to those addressed in the beginning of the epistle, including, of course, 'the church in your house'.

spiritually Thompson (1967) remarks that "'your spirit' is the same as 'you'." John Knox (1955), however, says, "The phrase makes explicit what is always implied: the grace of Christ is always spiritually discerned and spiritually received." The statement "'your spirit' is the same as 'you'" suggests synecdoche, where the part is substituted for the whole. The question, then, is whether 'spirit' here is to be taken in its primary meaning or as what is, in effect, a 'dead' figure. The fact that some commentators take it in its primary meaning shows that it is not fully recognized as a 'dead' figure. And for this reason it seems best to keep 'spirit' in some form in the propositionalization. In natural English this is probably better expressed by the use of 'spiritually' rather than 'spirit(s)': '*I pray that* the Lord Jesus Christ *will continue to* bless you(pl) spiritually'.

In some languages, however, it may be impossible or inappropriate to translate 'spiritually' or even 'spirit(s)' literally in this context, so 'you(pl)' may be substituted for 'your spirit(s)'.

BIBLIOGRAPHY

Commentaries and Other Studies Relating to Philemon

Alford, Henry. [1865] 1958. *Galatians–Philemon*. The Greek Testament, vol. 3. Reprint. Chicago: Moody Press.

Barclay, William. [1956] 1960. *The Letters to Timothy, Titus, and Philemon*. The Daily Study Bible. Reprint. Philadelphia: Westminster Press.

Barker, Kenneth, ed. 1985. *The NIV Study Bible*. Grand Rapids: Zondervan.

Beekman, John, and John Callow. 1974. *Translating the Word of God*. Grand Rapids: Zondervan.

Betz, Hans Dieter. 1975. "The Literary Composition and Function of Paul's Letter to the Galatians." *New Testament Studies* 21:353–79.

Calvin, John. [c. 1850]. *Commentary on Timothy, Titus, and Philemon*. Calvin's Commentaries. Calvin Translation Society, ed. [Edinburgh: T. & T. Clark.] Reprint. Grand Rapids: Baker. (Also Torrance, ed., vol. 10. Edinburgh: St. Andrews Press; Grand Rapids: Eerdmans.)

Carson, Herbert M. 1960. *The Epistles to the Colossians and to Philemon*. Tyndale New Testament Commentary. Grand Rapids: Eerdmans.

Ellicott, Charles J. 1865. *A Critical and Grammatical Commentary on St. Paul's Epistles to the Philippians, Colossians, and to Philemon*. Andover: Warren F. Draper.

Erdman, Charles R. 1933. *The Epistles of Paul to the Colossians and to Philemon*. Philadelphia: Westminster Press.

Failing, George E. 1966. "Philemon." *The Wesleyan Bible Commentary*. Grand Rapids: Eerdmans.

Farrar, Frederick W. 1895. *The Life and Work of St. Paul*. London, Paris, and Melbourne: Cassell & Co.

Field, Frederick. 1889. *Notes on the Translation of the New Testament*. Cambridge: Cambridge University Press.

Graham, Glenn H. 1983. *An Exegetical and Translation Handbook on Paul's Letter to Philemon*. Ukarumpa, Papua New Guinea: Summer Institute of Linguistics.

Greenlee, J. Harold. 1989. *An Exegetical Summary of Titus and Philemon*. Dallas: Summer Institute of Linguistics.

Guthrie, Donald. 1970. "Commentary on Philemon." In *The New Bible Commentary*. 3rd ed., ed. by D. Guthrie et al. London: InterVarsity Press; Grand Rapids: Eerdmans.

Hendriksen, William. 1964. *Exposition of Colossians and Philemon*. New Testament Commentary. Grand Rapids: Baker.

Knox, John. 1955. "The Epistle to Philemon." In *The Interpreter's Bible*, vol. 11. New York: Abingdon Press.

Knox, Ronald A. 1956. *New Testament Commentary*, vol. 3. London: Burns Oates.

Lenski, Richard C. H. [1937] 1946. *The Interpretation of St. Paul's Epistles to the Colossians, to the Thessalonians, to Timothy, to Titus, and to Philemon*. Reprint. Columbus: Wartburg Press.

Lightfoot, Joseph B. [1879] 1973. *St. Paul's Epistles to the Colossians and to Philemon*. Reprint. [London: Macmillan.] Grand Rapids: Zondervan.

Lohse, Eduard. [1968] 1971. *A Commentary on the Epistles to Colossians and to Philemon*. Tr. by William R. Poehlmann and Robert J. Karris. Ed. by Helmut Koester. Hermeneia. Philadelphia: Fortress Press.

Martin, Ralph P. 1974. *Colossians and Philemon*. New Century Bible. Greenwood, S.C.: Attic Press.

Meyer, Heinrich A. W. 1885. *Critical and Exegetical Handbook to the Epistles to the Philippians and Colossians, and to Philemon*. New York: Funk and Wagnalls.

Moule, C. F. D. 1958. *The Epistles of Paul the Apostle to the Colossians and to Philemon*. The Cambridge Greek Testament Commentary. Cambridge: Cambridge University Press.

Muller, Jac. J. 1955. *The Epistles of Paul to the Philippians and to Philemon*. The New International Commentary on the New Testament. Grand Rapids: Eerdmans.

Oesterley, W. E. 1910. "The Epistle to Philemon."" In *The Expositor's Greek Testament*, vol. 4. Reprint. Grand Rapids: Eerdmans.

Pope, Anthony G., et al. n.d. "A Literary-Semantic Analysis of Philemon." Prepublication draft. Dallas: Summer Institute of Linguistics.

Scott, E. G. 1930. "The Epistles of Paul to the Colossians, to Philemon and to the Ephesians." *The Moffatt New Testament Commentary*. New York: Harper & Row.

Sirpesteijn, P. J. 1979. "A Scribe at Work." *The Bulletin of the American Society of Papyrologists* 16:4.

Thompson, G. H. P. 1967. *The Letters of Paul to the Ephesians, to the Colossians and to Philemon*. The Cambridge Bible Commentary. Cambridge: Cambridge University Press.

Lange, John Peter. [1868] 1960. "The Epistle of Paul to Philemon," translated, with additions, by Horatio B. Hackett. In *Lange's Commentary on the Holy Scriptures*, vol. 11. Reprint. Grand Rapids: Zondervan.

Vincent, Marvin R. 1897. *A Critical and Exegetical Commentary on the Epistles to the Philippians and to Philemon*. The International Critical Commentary. Edinburgh: T. & T. Clark.

White, J. L. n.d. "The Structural Analysis of Philemon: A Point of Departure in the Formal Analysis of the Pauline Letter." *SBL 107th Annual Meeting Seminar Papers* 1:1–47.

Grammars, Lexicons, and Other Reference Works

Bauer, W., W. F. Arndt, and F. W. Gingrich. 1979. *A Greek-English Lexicon of the New Testament and other Early Christian Literature*. 2d. ed. Revised and augmented by F. W. Gingrich and F. W. Danker from Walter Bauer's 5th ed., 1958. Chicago: University of Chicago Press.

Banker, John. 1987. *A Semantic Structure Analysis of Titus*. Dallas: Summer Institute of Linguistics.

Beekman, John, John Callow, and Michael F. Kopesec. 1981. "The Semantic Structure of Written Communication." Prepublication draft, 5th ed. Dallas: Summer Institute of Linguistics.

Blass, F., and A. Debrunner. 1961. *A Greek Grammar of the New Testament and Other Early Christian Literature*. A translation and revision of the 9th-10th German edition by Robert W. Funk. Chicago: University of Chicago Press.

Bullinger, E. W. 1898. *Figures of Speech Used in the Bible*. London: Eyre and Spottiswoode.

Callow, John. 1982. *A Semantic Structure Analysis of Second Thessalonians*. Dallas: Summer Institute of Linguistics.

———. 1983. *A Semantic Structure Analysis of Colossians*. Dallas: Summer Institute of Linguistics.

Callow, Kathleen. 1998. *Man and Message*. Lanham, Maryland: University Press of America and Summer Institute of Linguistics.

Campbell, J. Y. 1932. "Koinōnia and its Cognates in the New Testament." *Journal of Biblical Literature* 51:352–80.

Dana, H. E., and Julius R. Mantey. 1957. *A Manual Grammar of the Greek New Testament*. New York: Macmillan.

Douglas, J. D., ed. 1962. *New Bible Dictionary*. London: InterVarsity Press; Grand Rapids: Eerdmans.

Friberg, Barbara, and Timothy Friberg. 1981. *Analytical Greek New Testament*. Grand Rapids: Baker.

Greenlee, J. Harold. 1986. *A Concise Exegetical Grammar of New Testament Greek*. 5th ed., revised. Grand Rapids: Eerdmans.

Guthrie, Donald. 1961. *New Testament Introduction*. London: InterVarsity Press.

Liddell, H. G., and R. Scott. 1968. *A Greek-English Lexicon*. 9th ed. with supplement, revised by H. S. Jones. Oxford: Oxford University Press.

McKay, K. L. 1972. "Syntax in Exegesis." *Tyndale Bulletin* 23.

Moule, C. F. D. 1963. *An Idiom-Book of New Testament Greek*. 2nd ed. Cambridge: Cambridge University Press.

Moulton, James H., and George Milligan. 1914-1929. *The Vocabulary of the Greek Testament Illustrated from the Papyri and Other Non-Literary Sources*. Reprint. Grand Rapids: Eerdmans.

Robinson, J. Armitage. 1909. *St. Paul's Epistle to the Ephesians*. London: Macmillan. Reprint. London: Kregel.

The Bible Translator. Journal published quarterly by the United Bible Societies.

The Reader's Digest Great Encyclopedic Dictionary. 1966. Pleasantville, New York: Reader's Digest Association.

Tuggy, John C. 1992. "Semantic Paragraph Patterns: A Fundamental Communication Concept and Interpretive Tool." *Linguistics and New Testament Interpretation*, ed. David Alan Black, pp. 45–67. Nashville, Tenn.: Broadman.

Turner, Nigel. 1963. Syntax. *A Grammar of New Testament Greek*, vol. 3. Edinburgh: T. & T. Clark.

Texts and Versions

Aland, Barbara, Kurt Aland, Johannes Karavidopoulos, Carlo M. Martini, and Bruce M. Metzger, eds. 1993. *The Greek New Testament*. 4th rev. ed. Stuttgart: United Bible Societies.

Aland, Kurt, Matthew Black, Carlo M. Martini, Bruce M. Metzger, and Allen Wikgren, eds. 1975. *The Greek New Testament*. 3d ed. Stuttgart: United Bible Societies.

Anderson, Julian G. 1984. *A New Accurate Translation of the Greek New Testament into Simple Everyday American English*. Dallas, Pa.: Offset Paperback Mfrs.

Beck, William F. 1963. *The New Testament in the Language of Today*. St. Louis: Concordia.

Berry, George Ricker. [1897] 1982. *Interlinear Greek-English New Testament*. [Reading, Pa.: Handy Book Co.] Reprint. Grand Rapids: Baker.

Bruce, F. F. 1965. *The Letters of Paul*. Grand Rapids: Eerdmans.

Good News Bible: The Bible in Today's English Version. 1976. New York: American Bible Society.

Goodspeed, Edgar J. 1923. *The New Testament: An American Translation*. Chicago: University of Chicago Press.

Hodges, Zane C., and Arthur L. Farstad, eds. 1985. *The Greek New Testament according to the Majority Text*. 2nd ed. Nashville: Thomas Nelson Publishers.

ἩΚΑΙΝΗ ΔΙΑΘΗΚΗ. 1904. London: British and Foreign Bible Society.

ἩΚΑΙΝΗ ΔΙΑΘΗΚΗ. 1958. 2nd ed. with revised critical apparatus (Nestle-Kirkpatrick). London: British and Foreign Bible Society.

The Holy Bible: Authorized (or King James) Version. 1611.

The Holy Bible: New International Version. 1978. New York: New York International Bible Society.

The Holy Bible: Revised Standard Version. 1953. New York: Thomas Nelson and Sons.

The Holy Bible: Revised Version. 1885. Oxford: Oxford University Press.

The Jerusalem Bible. 1966. Garden City: Doubleday.

Kleist, James A., and Joseph L. Lilly. 1956. *The New Testament*. Milwaukee: Bruce Publishing Co.

Knox, Ronald A. 1944. *The New Testament*. New York: Sheed and Ward.

Luther, Martin. n.d. *Die Heilige Schrift. Die Epistel S. Pauli: An Philemon*.

Moffatt, James. 1935. *A New Translation of the Bible*. Revised. New York: Harper.

The New American Standard Bible. 1963. La Habra: Foundation Press.

The New English Bible. 1961. Oxford: Oxford University Press; Cambridge: Cambridge University Press.

Norlie, Olaf M. 1961. *The New Testament: A Translation in Modern English for Today's Reader*. Grand Rapids: Zondervan.

Novum Testamentum Graece. 1947. 2nd ed. Ed. by A. Souter. Oxford: Oxford University Press.

Novum Testamentum Latine. 1911. Wordsworth and White, eds. Oxford: Clarendon Press.

Phillips, J. B. 1958. *The New Testament in Modern English*. New York: Macmillan.

Segond, Louis F. 1968. *La Sainte Bible*. Geneva: La Maison de la Bible.

Taylor, Kenneth N. 1971. *The Living Bible*. Wheaton: Tyndale House.

The Translator's New Testament. 1973. London: British and Foreign Bible Society.

The Twentieth Century New Testament. [1904] 1945. New York: Revell.

Verkuyl, Gerrit. 1969. *The Modern Language Bible*. Grand Rapids: Zondervan.

Dios Llega al Hombre: Version Popular. 1966. Sociedades Biblicas en America Latina.

Way, Arthur S. 1926. *Letters of St. Paul and Hebrews*. 6th ed. London: Macmillan.

Weymouth, Richard Francis. [1929] 1943. *The New Testament in Modern Speech*. 5th ed., revised by J. A. Robertson. Boston: Pilgrim Press.

Williams, Charles B. 1963. *The New Testament in the Language of the People*. Chicago: Moody Press.

Williams, Charles Kingsley. 1952. *The New Testament: A New Translation in Plain English*. London: S. P. C. K. and Longmans, Green and Co.

ISBN: 0-88312-934-5

www.ingramcontent.com/pod-product-compliance
Lightning Source LLC
Chambersburg PA
CBHW082207230426
43672CB00015B/2925